Books are to be returned on or before
the last date below.

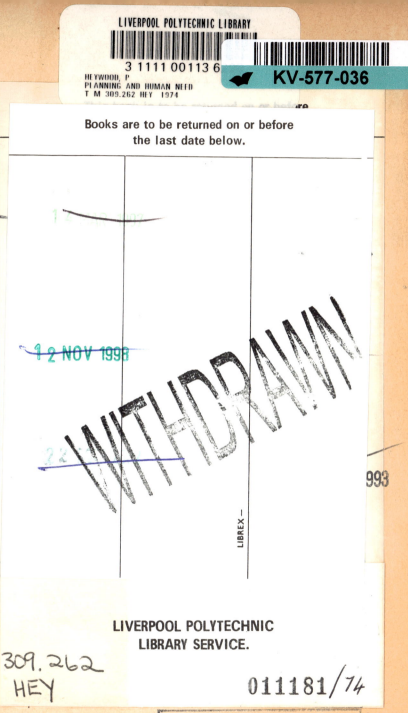

1 2 NOV 1998

993

LIBREX —

WITHDRAWN

PLANNING AND HUMAN NEED

PEOPLE, PLANS AND PROBLEMS SERIES

General editor: Professor J. B. Mays
Department of Sociology
University of Liverpool

Others in the series

PLANNING
AND HUMAN NEED

PHIL HEYWOOD

David & Charles *Newton Abbot*

To Mum and Dad, with love

0 7153 6315 8

Set in 11 on 13 point Baskerville
and printed in Great Britain
by John Sherratt and Son Ltd   Altrincham
for David & Charles (Holdings) Limited
South Devon House Newton Abbot Devon

Contents

Acknowledgements

I should like to thank all the many friends and colleagues who have given generously of that most valuable commodity, their time, to discuss the ideas and read the text of this book, in particular Ian Crowther, Martin Jordan, Steve Leach and John Young. I am also indebted to Murdoch Mactaggart for advice on questions of social change and political organisation, Don Simpson on housing matters, Jon Allison on pedestrian movement in town centres, and John Taylor on Community Action. I am grateful to Roger McGough for permission to use his poem *M66*, and to Michael Young and Peter Willmott for allowing me to reprint material on the Londoner's spending priorities. I should add that I owe the development of many of my ideas on planning and society to contact with students and community groups in Liverpool.

I should like to thank Mrs Beryl Mackintosh for her expert typing, consistent interest and suggestions, and valuable assistance with spelling and punctuation; and my wife, Sheila, for her willing reading of many drafts of each chapter, and for her consistently perceptive and constructive criticism. Finally, I must thank Professor John Mays for his unfailing guidance and encouragement, without which this book would not have been completed.

P.H.

6

Foreword

One of the difficulties in writing about any of the aspects of planning is that the word means different things to different people. To the alert citizen, interested in the many changes affecting the society in which he lives, it will probably include proposals for a wide range of physical developments (such as roads, housing and industrial estates, shopping and community centres, hospitals, schools, and even social facilities). To the member of some underprivileged group, such as an old person in a slum-clearance area, it may conjure up the working of a vast and impersonal government machine intent upon depriving him of his home, without any guarantee that he will like the alternative being offered, or be able to adapt to it if he does not. To the business executive, planning is both the process of plotting his firm's future success and growth, and also the apparatus (which he may resent) of government controls, set up to protect the public interest, inside which he must work.

The professional town and country planner concentrates on a particular aspect of physical planning—the allocation of suitable sites for particular activities—and he is often pained that the dissatisfaction caused by badly conceived or designed features like tower blocks of flats, or new housing estates with inadequate social facilities, should be directed at him. It may seem surprising that an activity with such an apparently wide

7

range should, in fact, be confined to the seemingly narrow role of suggesting land uses.

Yet it is clear that no one group of specialists could or should exert control over all the diverse developments generated in modern mass societies; such an attempt could only result in the worst kind of authoritarianism. For a set of professionals to be able to dictate how other people should live would be intolerable. A line must be drawn between matters having far-reaching social implications, where regulation is necessary to prevent one man's liberty trespassing on that of his neighbours, and others that are largely questions of personal choice of life-style and beliefs, and in which there should be no interference with the individual. For example, it may be a legitimate planning decision to recommend how much housing land should be released, and in what areas, but the type and design of dwellings must be questions of personal preference, and should only be decided after consultation with the future residents, and preferably with their participation in outlining their requirements. This leads us to yet one more view of planning, that of the advocate whose concern is to help particular disadvantaged groups work out their own solutions, and win government support to implement them.

The theme of this book is that only through consultation in strategic decisions, and participation in local ones, can planning achieve sufficiently firm anchorages to prevent it from drifting into manipulation and autocracy. In planning for the health of cities, there can be only one reliable consultant, and that is the citizen himself.

P.H.

1 The Urban Paradox

There is no avoiding the mounting problems of our cities. The many who live within them daily encounter congestion on streets and pavements, contamination of the air, and incessant destruction of familiar environments. Services such as public housing, refuse collection, policing, and even education are facing breakdown. Inequality, and antagonism between groups, are frequently fuelled by administrative failure and bureaucratic remoteness. Yet it is the modern city which has produced, and is maintaining, western man's unparalleled mastery over his environment, bringing together the ideas and activities of many specialists to enable groups to extend a joint domination over their environment that would be beyond them as individuals. This is the urban paradox, that modern cities are threatened by the very growth which their success has made possible. What is the nature of this growth, and how has it given rise to our current problems?

Both the explosion of human population of the last 200 years and the increasing proportion of that total living in towns and cities can be shown to stem from the same root cause—the increased mastery over the environment made possible by historically recent developments of scientific knowledge. On the one hand food supplies have been increased by the use of scientific farming methods; on the other the depredations of endemic

9

disease and plague have been sharply reduced by the introduction of preventive medicine.

Traditionally the city has been a much unhealthier place than the countryside, and cities formerly accommodated only a small proportion of the population, despite receiving continuous flows of immigrants in search of fame and fortune.[1] Now the new-found healthiness of the city has removed the most effective check on its growth, at the very moment when the vastly increased productive power of modern technology has redoubled its attractions to rural immigrants, who are themselves surviving in much greater numbers, and are unable to find work in their home villages.

Recent Growth of Cities

Today thirty times as many people live in cities with populations of 100,000 or more as did in 1800, though total world population has only trebled.[2] There are over 100 cities with populations of a million persons or more, and they exist in all six continents. There is a similarly wide distribution of intermediate-size cities with a population greater than 100,000. In the UK, USA, Germany, Japan and Australia more than a third of the total live in such cities, whose growth is taking place most rapidly in the least urbanised countries.[3] Western Europe is in the middle of a second urban revolution, whose initial, and perhaps most nightmarish, phase has been faithfully followed in each of the other continents: first by North America in the second half of the nineteenth century, a progress tellingly chronicled by the admirable school of so-called 'urban muckrakers' led by Josiah Strong,[4] Lincoln Steffens, and Upton Sinclair (who clearly expressed his view of Chicago in 1906 in The Jungle). The familiar ingredients of exploitation, disease, poverty and conflict were here made more poignant by the pathetically high hopes of many of the new inhabitants of these cities, fleeing from the injustice and penury of life in rural Europe.

We are at present confronted by the tragic spectacle of South America, Africa, and Asia passing through this stage of uncontrolled growth, as the horrors of disease, overcrowding and poverty in such widely separated cities as Lagos, Calcutta, Ankara, Lima and Rio de Janeiro testify.

The failure of the nineteenth-century European and North American cities, and their twentieth-century counterparts in Asia, South America and Africa, to provide decent living standards for their citizens stems from the same three basic difficulties that are bedevilling western cities today. Firstly there is the inability either to control technology, or to adapt to it. Secondly, there is the problem of achieving rapid growth without a lowering in standards of housing and environment. Thirdly, there is a dangerous unwillingness on the part of the well established few to acknowledge the demands of all to share equally in the prosperity of their common city.

If the nineteenth-century city fathers made no attempt to prevent the introduction of steam-powered mills into the heart of ancient cathedral cities, nor do we take effective steps to keep the equally dirty and even more dangerous motor car out of *our* city centres. If they allowed noxious emissions from chemical works to foul their waterways, we do the same on a grander scale. If they tore down the finest parts of their cities to make way for expanding commerce, irrespective of whether it could equally well be diverted elsewhere, so do we.

Great as were the problems of rapid urban growth which resulted from the high tide of the Industrial Revolution, they were no more challenging that those facing the twentieth-century city as its role is transformed from being the *centre* for a densely populated hinterland to the actual *container* for the vast majority of the total population. Over 90 per cent of the population of the UK already lives in settlements classed as urban, and most of the rest are clustered round in suburbs.[5] Although modern conurbations may have grown up from forty or fifty different townships, administered from twenty or thirty different town halls, in many respects they function as single economic organisms, demanding an entirely new approach to planning and city government. In the United States they are not getting it, and in the UK the proposed reorganisation is poor and partial.[6]

Such failures create their own costs. The violence of the nineteenth-century city stemmed from the resentment and deprivation of the urban proletariat, and the pattern is being repeated in Chicago and Belfast, Reggio Calabria and Montevideo.[7] The city is an incomparable productive unit, but the inevitable price of this efficiency is interdependence. Even the Victorian industrialists were forced to recognise this when they finally supported legislation against the appalling housing and medical conditions of the workers, which brought the spectre of cholera into the city.[8] The investing and middle classes of the present are no readier to share the common wealth equally with the labouring classes. But because the city depends upon mutual co-operation between *all* its workers and residents, there is a limit to the extent to which even quite small minorities can be exploited. Groups of disaffected individuals (such as New York lift operatives, and London refuse collectors) can upset the entire urban system. The modern city may survive without social justice, but it will not prosper.

John Lindsay, when Mayor of New York, recently outlined the problems which confront his city, and many others.[9] Underlying many of them he sees the twin issues of mounting costs as the existing urban structure becomes increasingly incapable of meeting modern demands; and alienation of individuals and groups from each other and the metropolis as a whole, as they sense their powerlessness in its expanding scale. Solutions must be sought inside two general strategies. New physical structures, capable of dealing with mass demands, must be funded and introduced; and there must be continuous consultation to discover the needs and priorities of the specific groups who will be using these facilities. Modernisation can be made sensitive to social needs.

Most important of all the sense of identification of the individual with his community must be strengthened, for the good of both. Just as the house that is owned by its occupiers

is often improved by maintenance and decoration, and beauti-
fied by planting, while a house felt to be someone else's property
may slip into rapid decay, so also with districts and neighbourhoods. As alienation, apathy and neglect go hand in hand, so
do participation and improvement.

The problems of alienation are not only political and economic, but also psychological. There is a deep-seated hostility and
suspicion of cities in many western nations, and it is frequently
shared by city dwellers themselves. It is based on a view of the
city as the centre of the web of bureaucracy, and the seat of
dominating elites, devouring and exploiting the surrounding
countryside and its people.

But there have also been epochs when cities have been
bastions of freedom for serfs against their feudal landlords, and
of urban proletariats against exploiting elites.[10] Now that
theoretical democracy has opened at least the prospect of
government by consent, and public-health reform has raised
life expectancy in most great cities to levels close to the national
average, its two greatest traditional failings have been removed.

Preservation of its vitality is important because the city is
the focus of a civilisation—the place of contact and confrontation, the nursery of new ideas, and the forcing house of new
developments. Man's dominance, based on his ability to cooperate in production, is often spurred by a desire to compete
in consumption; and the city is the ideal stage for both competition and cooperation. Its concentration of people and buildings ensures ease of exchange of goods and ideas; the existence
of institutions such as markets, guilds, and schools provides
continuity and stable regulation; a central position at the focus
of existing routes favours collection of raw materials and distribution of products; and finally the urban stage itself, with
its dense population, and cultural traditions and facilities, constitutes a unique setting for the social life of a gregarious species.

Physical Problems of Cities

No physical problems are more noticeable than the decay and

congestion of the older parts of major cities, many of whose overcrowded dwellings were built as near-slums in the second half of the nineteenth century to house low-paid industrial workers with no choice. Once these are cleared, there is no reason why the later artisans' housing, constructed under public-health regulations, and local bylaws, should not be repaired and maintained as a valuable and often attractive part of the city's housing stock.

There is public dismay at the ugliness and sheer size of much new central-area development. Every day the city seems to become less *our* city, and more that of the machine. The gigantic scale and impersonal design of many new developments must tend to shake our confidence in ourselves as human beings, and alienate us from our own cities. The rate at which shopping and office 'precincts', tower blocks of flats, 'civic centres' and monstrous urban motorways are being constructed is such that we must act quickly if the cities are not to become petrified forests of concrete slabs and podiums.

The most obvious reason for their rapid spread, of course, lies in the desire to make the most profitable use of very central, and thus valuable, locations, a desire shared by developers and by local councils (which wish to achieve the highest possible rateable values). Whether or not it would be more advantageous for the city to have a wider spread of high value uses, resulting in less congestion, and fewer tall buildings in town centres is a matter of opinion. But it is not the existence of a few very tall buildings in the heart of the city that is at question—it is the supine acceptance by planners and councillors that such buildings are the norm for *all* new development in the town centre, and that only existing buildings of outstanding achitectural merit shall be protected from replacement by this kind of intimidating slab.

Technological determinism and architectural fashion are also playing their parts. For the past 100 years many avant-garde designers and engineers have worked on the principle that every technical invention or innovation should be utilised to the full;

they then argued, under the banners of functionalism and 'honesty', that the design of structures and cities should be dictated by the potential of materials and machines, and not the needs of their occupants or users.[11] Obvious examples of this tendency can be found in the design of open-plan dwellings, which are very unsuitable for families, following on the development of cheap, light steel girders capable of spanning the width of an entire house;[12] the use of box-girder construction for bridges, dangerously lowering safety standards; the stacking of precast components into tower blocks like London's Ronan Point;[13] and the craze amongst municipal architects themselves to put up tall buildings to provide 'visual emphasis' in their towns. The heart of the problem is that as we gain increasing mastery over the use of materials and machines, the scale on which it is possible to build, the scale therefore attractive to the architect, engineer, and developer, becomes even larger. The planner, deeply embedded in the same culture, milieu and possibly even organisation as his co-professionals, often takes recourse in private grief rather than effective prevention.

There are two other critical causes for the ugliness and inhumanity of much new development which will form themes throughout this book. They are the failure to consult with present and future users, and the lack of any precise definition of objectives and examination of alternative ways of fulfilling them. Thousands of millions of pounds and dollars have been spent on building huge new pedestrianised shopping precincts in both Western Europe and North America; yet there has been little or no consultation with shoppers in the cities concerned as to whether they wanted the old centres torn down and replaced; or where they would like new shops to be situated; or how designed; or of what types. Instead, universal and brutal two- or three-level concrete anthills have been thrust down in the heart of cities, driving out small specialist shops and thriving local concerns alike, and dislocating both movement and contact. The developers profit, because the market is rigged, by parking regulations and provisions, and routing of public transport, in favour of the new shops. The city corporation and the more affluent ratepayers profit because of the rates paid by the new concerns; but the people whose notional advantage has been used to justify the whole scheme—the city's shoppers—have been given neither power nor choice in the decision. If the scale of these new developments is not humane, it is because their objectives are not; if their architecture pays no respect to the existing character of the city, it is of little concern to their designers, who view themselves as national or international characters rather than members of one particular city; if the shoppers in them are silent, abstracted, and frequently appear confused, it is because the development has not been designed for their convenience, and a degree of confusion may even increase their propensity to spend uncritically.

This cynicism is often abetted by fashions in design and by ignorance. A dimly felt need is sensed intuitively—whether for more recreation, shops, or public buildings—and a solution is invented. Even at the outset the objectives are not clearly defined; soon they are completely lost sight of, in the enthusiastic advocacy of the new proposal, and the listing of all the new benefits it will convey. Of course nothing is done to discover if these benefits are in fact what the supposed beneficiaries want, or if they are, whether they are willing to pay the required cost; or whether the same or greater benefits could be achieved more cheaply by an alternative scheme. The whole project is swept forward with the zeal of the visionary. It is inevitable that designers fall in love with their own creations—but it is arguable that planners are paid by the community to evaluate their rhetoric more coolly, using the criteria of the preferences and stated needs of the individuals and groups who will be most affected.

Economic Problems

One of the great paradoxes of the mid-twentieth century in the United States is of course the fact that the society that is at once the richest, and one of the most urbanised, in the history of civilisation should be plagued by the threat, and in many cases the reality, of urban bankruptcy.[14] The reasons are not economic—the American city has not ceased to be a wonderfully effective productive unit—but social and political. Tides of impoverished and unskilled rural immigrants continue to flow into the heart of the great industrial cities of the north-east and California, from the deep south, in search of work, creating constantly greater demands on all urban services; and at the same time the more affluent and successful residents move out beyond the city limits to high-class residential neighbourhoods with lower rates, more attractive environments, and fewer social problems, thus depriving the city of financial support and local leadership, but in most cases continuing to rely on it for cultural, social, commercial and industrial services.[15] As a result, money gets scarcer, services deteriorate further, and more of those who can afford to do so leave. This process is reinforced by the policy of the Federal Housing Administration of channelling money into house building by keeping mortgage rates low for home owners, and guaranteeing their loans.[16] Public housing is regarded as an unfortunate public liability rather than a major instrument of housing policy.[17] Thus is the urban trap constructed. The spring mechanism is the freedom of suburban councils to fix their own zoning regulations so low that only the rich can afford to buy their way into them, leaving the poor and the black where they started—in the ghetto. Of course this problem is, like most others affecting the city, capable of a political solution.

Friedman has suggested a form of single regional government to supersede the present pattern of separate local governments for the central ghetto and the surrounding garden suburbs.[18] Mayor Lindsay said he would be happy to see a redrawing of city boundaries, and a juster sharing of power between city and state.[19] Designation of metropolitan physical development agencies on the same basis as those recently established in France has also been advocated.[20] Neither of the two major political parties has shown the slightest interest in implementing any of these reforms, which would detract from the political power of their existing machines in ways that would threaten the established positions of thousands of party stalwarts and activists. In many ways the black militants in the cities are only voicing the attitude of the national power elite when they cry 'Burn, baby, burn!' Perhaps there is a dawning awareness that by concentrating the most impoverished and ill-educated in the central cities, and then refusing them necessary funds, the USA could do itself irreparable harm, but so far this has only expressed itself in presidential rhetoric and promises.

Elsewhere the situation is not yet so serious. In Asia, Africa, and South America, the cities, impoverished as they often are, are generally less so than the surrounding countryside. In parts of Western Europe, however, particularly in the United Kingdom, there are incipient signs of the same difficulties. The existence of over 1,200 local authorities in the UK, with a patchwork of interlocking powers and areas, is no less anachronistic than the situation in the USA. The Conservative government elected in 1970 decided not to accept the recommendations for reform made by the Royal Commission appointed by the previous Labour government, whereby the existing ramshackle structure would be replaced by fewer than eighty large all-purpose authorities, each more or less including a central city and its hinterland.[21]

There are, instead, to be two levels of local government, with numbers of districts, each with about 100,000 residents, grouped to form counties. The division of functions between the two is very blurred, but the decisive power in housing, planning and, most important of all, rate collection, is to be left in the hands of the local districts.[22] The scene is set for the same story—Garden Cities Round the Ghetto—as in the USA. Added to this, the splitting of such basically indivisible activities between different levels of authority is likely to be neither flexible nor efficient.

The absolute shortages of cash long experienced by American cities may soon occur in British ones as well, as the reduction of public spending becomes one of the major priorities of central government. The large proportion of local-government funds that comes from the national exchequer—over a half—has traditionally provided a useful means of maintaining central control, and there is no intention of relaxing this control. Local authorities are not to be allowed, as they are in the USA, to levy taxes on car licences, petrol or income; they are not even to be allowed to run municipal lotteries.[23]

If cities are to have the funds and authority necessary to solve their problems, however, three conditions must be fulfilled:

1. administrative boundaries must be redrawn to include all the areas which rely on the city for their economic existence;

2. central government must contribute block grants on a sliding scale to those cities suffering from excessively low per capita incomes;

3. local authorities should be empowered to use local taxation to raise funds, and to control urban development.

Social Problems in the Pressure Areas

From its very beginnings the city has been a place of conflict as well as contact. Today that conflict is becoming more overt and continuous, both between classes and racial groups. Where channels of communication, negotiation and progress become blocked, the result is often violence. Established and prosperous groups may associate this with the arrival of particular minorities, not realising that the secret of the city's remarkable economic success lies in its open-ness and, in part, in the continuous infusion of new citizens with new ideas. A stagnant city is neither a desirable nor a practicable proposition. The advent of gunpowder, and the eventual extinction of the walled city, made the exclusion of rural migrants impossible; and once people are inside the city it is dangerous to drive them to desperation. There is no escaping the conclusion that in the modern city we must sink or swim together. We must identify and tackle our social problems.

Foremost among these are the existence of large impoverished minorities, the prevalence of crime, and a mounting sense of isolation and alienation among many who are neither poor nor criminal.

The old fashioned equation between crime and poverty still exists in areas where there is multi-deprivation—of education, environment, housing, job opportunities, cultural development and levels of aspiration. This culture of poverty—concentrated, corrosive, and self-perpetuating—is the most basic and painful of the problems of the modern city, all the more bitter because it exists in close contact with the showy affluence of the city's central department stores, car showrooms and gaudy travel agents. The problems of poverty in the city are exacerbated, as are those of crime, by the tendency of like people to be clustered together. Just as the affluent are drawn to the spacious suburbs, with their gardens, parks and golf courses, so are the impoverished pushed inexorably into the inner ring of decaying nineteenth-century mansions, now converted into lodging houses. Discomfort, difficulty in meeting high rentals, and a pervading sense of discontent cause tenants to make repeated moves within this area, which is sometimes termed the zone of transition. Stable families are less common than casual liaisons. The dividing line between looseness and prostitution is often blurred, and children are brought up with severely limited expectations of themselves and others.

At night time in the summer such areas have a certain seedy glamour, with children playing out in the dusk as the other members of the household come home from the pub. The place at least seems lively in contrast with the silent and private night-time world of the outer suburbs. But on a winter's morning the reality is laid bare. Lonely and fatherless families wake up in rooms stinking of excrement because the youngest child has used his pot in the night and it is two flights of stairs to the nearest lavatory. Dampness is oozing through the peeling wallpaper. There is little food in the house, and breakfast consists of a slice of bread and margarine. What men there are in the street (since women predominate) emerge hollow-eyed and coughing from the damp houses to go to their jobs on building sites, if they are lucky, and if not, to wait for the betting shop and later the pubs to open. Ill-clad children walk silently through the streets on their way to school; in many cases the lack of childish high spirits is due to a sleepless night disturbed by the coughing of other children sharing the same room, or the rough and tumble taking place on the mother's bed.

Impressive three- and four-storey terraces of classical town houses, each with nine or ten large and high-ceilinged rooms, originally intended for occupation by single families, their children and servants, are now forced to provide accommodation for as many as fifty people in ten separate households. Work done by Steve Leach and myself in 1969 in Manchester's Moss Side indicated a widespread lack of even the most basic facilities: one dwelling in eighteen had no access to even a cold-water tap; one in three had only shared use; and the same proportion had to share the use of a lavatory. Since overcrowding was also very prevalent, with six times as many people living at two persons or more to a room than in the rest of the city, the reality of discomfort, inconvenience and squalor can be imagined.[24] This situation has been described by the Medical Officer of Health for the fashionable London Borough of Kensington, in his evidence to the UK Government Royal Commission on London's housing problem. He refers to . . .

> The herding together of people, often incompatible. The inconveniences, the lack of space especially for such things as playing or pram storage, the inadequate and inconvenient washing, sanitary and food handling facilities, stairs, noise, fetching and carrying distances, dilapidation and depressing appearance of parts used in common.[25]

The irony of the situation is that the buildings themselves are often aesthetically among the most beautiful in the city, designed for the urban aristocracy of the nineteenth century. All that is needed is money to convert them to their modern role of lodging houses (to which they are structurally fairly well suited) and to restore and maintain the abundant open space with which they are endowed. Otherwise they will become slums.

It will be readily seen that these urban transit camps must imbue their permanent residents with a sense of hopelessness,

and enforced inferiority. Thus it is when the means of escape
are closed for particular groups—racial minorities, unskilled and
frequently unemployed workers, unmarried mothers—that the
rigours of the transit camp, uncomfortable but temporary, take
on the permanent and intolerable characteristics of a vice squeezing them between deteriorating housing and rising rents. Once
the vice is correctly perceived as being the urban system itself,
the most apparent alternatives are gutless surrender or urban
insurrection. Should the reasons for the riots which are tearing
apart cities in North and South America be sought in the conditions to which the people of such inner areas and favellas
(South American shanty towns) are subjected, and not in their
racial or social character?

The problems of European cities are smaller because the
numbers of underprivileged migrants are less, but they are clearly
evident—nowhere more so at the moment than in Ulster. In
the great cities of Italy and Britain the writing is clearly on the
slum and ghetto walls. Commonsense as well as compassion
demand a planning policy for the inner city, and for the underprivileged and unestablished who are at present forced to
congregate there.

In this problem, as in so many others that confront the city,
the basic issue is the willingness of each group, particularly the
most affluent, to realise that the continued existence of the city
life from which they benefit most depends on either the willing
cooperation, or the crude suppression, of every other group in
the city. The price the established middle classes must pay for
urban peace is urban justice, and it is a cost that must be paid
in many ways: in increased rates and taxes; the equalisation of
urban services; positive discrimination on behalf of the poor in
the housing market; subsidised services such as public transport;
and most fundamental of all, acceptance of greatly increased
competition in the cherished white-collar sector from the poor
and the alien—black, brown, rural and proletarian. There are
no good reasons why they should constitute a permanent cheap
labour force to do the dirty jobs of the city at cut rates.

2 *The Social Impact of Technological Change*

Much of the inequality lying at the heart of the problems of decay and conflict of the modern city stems from the very specialisation which has helped to foster its growth. The role, status, and income of individuals all tend to be decided by their possession of certain skills, or membership of particular groups, all set upon diverging courses. The less privileged are unable to improve their position relative to the better off, because their weaker economic position is reinforced by inferior education, less effective political organisation and exclusion from the decision-making processes. These problems are made more acute in western industrialised societies by the momentum of economic growth, competitive consumption and inflation, which continually outstrip attempts at redistribution of wealth. Even political leaders of parties formally committed to social justice invariably argue that the best way of raising the standards of living of the most underprivileged is for an extra effort to increase the *gross* national product, the formula for which is normally to export more, by holding production costs and wages down, thus imposing further financial sacrifices on the poorest members of society.

The relevance of this is that the city is a map of the economic strength of its people. Cramped and inadequate dwellings reflect cramped and inadequate incomes, and in turn give rise to lower levels of political effectiveness, weakening the possibility of a political solution to the cycle of poverty. Mitigating legislation only has been passed.

Specialisation and Social Inequality

Specialisation not only gives rise to classes; it also increases the absolute power of the city's rulers over the rest of society because they are in physical control of the places of work and exchange, and of the supplies of raw materials and finished products. Each new development of technology, such as iron smelting or the introduction of the wheel, has not only given rise to a new caste of specialists, possessed of greater economic power than the remaining non-specialists, but has also increased the absolute domination which rulers and elites can exert over the total population. In modern times ruling elites have come increasingly to rely on the support of people possessed of particular organisational, scientific, and high technological specialisms, and much greater rewards have been allotted to them than to others. A complex pattern of stratification has come to pervade all aspects of life from childhood to the grave. It rests on an implicit but circular value system in which rewards should be decided relative to social contribution, though social contribution is often judged by the reward which it is capable of commanding. Thus it is accepted that an advertising executive should receive a higher income than a dustman, though the value of the latter to society is incomparably greater.

Role allocation starts young: by the time children leave school they have been conditioned to accept a clear view of their career prospects, and provided with the necessary skills. This situation is reinforced by further education, which separates the more able or ambitious from the less. Expectations of future income also cause the life-styles and living areas of different groups to diverge from the beginning of their working lives. The university graduate will take out a mortgage and buy a house in an attractive and spacious suburb. In Western Europe the artisan undergoing training will enter his name on a council housing list, or start saving for a deposit to enter the private housing system at a later date, and in a less fashionable area. The semi-skilled or manual worker may try to obtain a council tenancy, or he may seek cheaper accommodation in the inner area of his city, probably close to his parents whose relatively deprived life-style is the one familiar to him. A large proportion of such families do not have private transport, and many, such as dustmen, waiters and shift workers, have to start work so early that they are unwilling to take houses at relatively high rents on outlying public housing estates. Thus the old houses of inner areas come to be occupied by low-income families, with relatively limited aspirations, who feel little incentive to improve or maintain dwellings which are not their own; also their relatively weak political organisation does not allow them to influence local government to raise the environmental and social facilities to the standard expected in the outer suburbs, occupied by professional and managerial people.

Such inequality of provision affects schools, parks and play spaces, libraries and street cleansing. Where certain much-valued facilities do exist, such as wash-houses and public baths, council officials living in the middle-class suburbs tend to regard the necessary subsidisation as proof that they are no longer needed, and should therefore be closed.

The processes whereby pay is settled reinforce this divergence of advantage. Clerical and administrative groups tend to see themselves as the paymasters because they earn more, and therefore pay higher taxes; the unskilled worker is seen, and often sees himself, as the recipient of 'their' wages. This problem is heightened by the fact that he has little security of employment, is frequently out of a job, and therefore must often rely on unemployment pay, and welfare or social security payments, all of which are kept under active surveillance by the press, and the professional and office elites, who are able to recruit large numbers of the less perceptive of the disadvantaged classes to decry their own associates for 'selfishness' in seeking to improve their position by demanding higher incomes. Meanwhile professional and managerial salaries continue quietly to rise at a faster rate, sometimes justified by the argument 'there are so few of us that it will make no difference to the national economy'. Professional specialists in administration quite naturally seek to ensure for themselves a disproportionately large amount of the national wealth, and allocate to other skilled specialists who might have the knowledge, organisation or power to dislodge them, lesser, but still considerable advantages over the least effective and powerful groups.

This process of social fission does not seem to be confined to capitalist societies, but operates wherever rapid increases in output are sought through increasing specialisation of labour and use of technical innovation. The criterion by which society is judged becomes national production, even though this may originally have been viewed as a means to achieving greater social justice. Because the significance of an individual is reduced to his contribution to output, he may be regarded as less important than the machine he operates. Unless the social divisiveness inherent in specialisation is counteracted, it seems that the individual must react in one of two ways. Either he must learn to love the machine that is working him, as Winston Smith did in Orwell's *1984*, and become alienated from his human decision-taking self, or he must alienate himself from the machine and seek to destroy it.

The tenor of this argument is not that the division of labour and the impact of technological development are unmitigated curses, but that they are mixed blessings, greatly expanding man's communal power over his environment at the same time as increasing society's existing tendencies towards exploitation and conflict. Because planners are charged with the problem of maintaining the health of the city, they should use every means at their disposal to ensure a fair balance of public services between groups, so that the inherently divisive forces involved are constantly corrected by a redistribution of public benefits to the disadvantaged.

There are two fundamental justifications for this, both concerned with equilibrium. Firstly, the environment is in itself educational: the messages we receive from the world we live in are stronger and deeper than those we receive in school. At present the low specialist groups are condemned to live in drab and often dangerous environments, learning lessons of group and individual exploitation, perceiving work as at best a necessary evil, and society as a game of rigged roulette. It is arguably part of town planning's job to change that picture by providing an equality of physical provisions throughout the city for housing, work, recreation, movement, and education.

Secondly, it is clear that specialisation and its attendant technology depend just as much on willing cooperation, and exchange of goods between specialists, as they do on the competitive urge to increase production and wealth. The great cities, dams, roads, and factories, for instance, which man has stamped on the face of the earth are all the result of human cooperation.

Technology and Values

Specialisation has been greatly fostered and accentuated by successive technological inventions, but it is doubtful whether technology is the sole or even the dominating determinant of all social organisation, as is held by numbers of American theorists like Webber, McLuhan and Meier.[1] Such technological determinists tend to argue that since everything else in society is conditioned by the prevailing productive techniques, attempts to control technological change are 'narrow and negative' and doomed to failure. This then leads on to an advocacy of 'predictive planning'—guessing the way that technology is likely to go—and attempting to change existing social and physical organisation to accommodate it. Those who take an opposite view argue that historically technology has as often been a product of a particular social situation, and the values held by its dominant elites, as the cause of them, and that it is not only possible but desirable to control its future development.

The argument is an important one, because of the enormous implications it has for the kind of society, and the kind of planning, which we want to achieve. The technological determinist would interpret history as the record of the cumulative impact of such technical inventions as the wheel, the plough, the printing press, the steam engine, the blast furnace, television, the internal combustion engine, nuclear fission and solid state electronics; and the growth of towns as the result of increasing levels of production and ease of communication. The enormous impact an invention may have upon ideas and organisations has been examined in detail by McLuhan, who shows how the use of the printing press encouraged the growth of the incipient bureaucracy on which the growing nation states depended, and fostered the growth of the elites which have continued to dominate western society.[2] He sees the advent of modern electronic mass media as destined to exert a similarly potent influence. For him 'the medium is the message'.[3]

Beguiling as such theories are, they are fundamentally superficial. Given that inventions are influential, one must ask what conditions give rise to them. Either these lie within the prevailing values, power structure or economic organisation of the fostering society, or the inventions are themselves unique 'first causes', akin to Darwin's concept of completely random genetic mutations. In this case, there must be some equivalent of a process of natural selection, deciding which ones shall survive and which be abandoned, and such a process must be decided by the values held by the particular society in which it occurs. The invention of a steam engine by Hero of Alexandria in 100 BC, for instance, did not develop into an industrial revolution in the speculative and non-materialistic Hellenic Egypt of that time. It seems that technical innovations are shaped by prevailing conditions and values. Some form of social control is certainly possible.

In an era as intellectually fertile as our own this process of control needs to be explicit and self-conscious. Leaving the process to take its course will result in a number of extremely unattractive and disfunctional developments being born, and only discarded after they have proved their uselessness or harmfulness. One well known current example is the lead additives which increase the performance of motor cars at the cost of producing deadly pools of poisonous pollution in the air of city streets.[4] The heedless rush to use rigid-frame and system-building techniques to erect high tower blocks to house council tenants has been even more disastrous in terms of adult anxiety and neurosis, and adolescent frustration and deprivation. The unregulated use of potentially beneficial inventions such as DDT and hormone insecticides has given equally harmful results, with large stretches of inland water like Lake Erie being partially sterilised, and increasing lengths of rivers all over Western Europe and North America being poisoned. In each case the mistake has resulted from an inability or unwillingness to plan technological developments in accord with the need and values of the time.

It is increasingly accepted that some form of control must be exerted over technology. But what should be the criterion? In the past it has been simple profitability to the practitioner, in the West, and in the Communist world contribution to the State's 5 year plan. In the current debate between the protagonists of economic growth and redistribution of wealth, conflicting suggestions are being made: on the one hand, increasing the gross national product and the absolute level of available wealth; on the other, a more stable balance between society and its environment, more equal shares of wealth for all, greater concentration on meeting basic human needs, and the provision of public as against private goods. Such a debate should provide politicians, planners, and technologists with a framework for selecting the areas for future investment, research and development.[5]

Growth and Redistribution of Wealth
It is clear that the two approaches are mutually incompatible. The higher levels of public investment in industry, and industrial services, which are necessary to achieve increased output, can only result from a diversion of resources away from non-

productive assistance to the poorer sections of the community. As we should expect, sharply rising levels of gross national product are usually, in fact, accompanied by widening gaps between the relative prosperity of the rich and the poor.[6]

The attempt to solve deprivation by growth also contains its own inbuilt momentum; when workers like miners, railwaymen and public-service employees complain that their already small portion of the national cake is being reduced in size relative to other groups (and by inflation), they are urged to increase their productivity so that national output can be expanded and they can, therefore, maintain their present standard of living with an even smaller share of the total cake.

It must be accepted that redistribution of wealth would slow down economic growth. Massive concentration of money in a few hands provides pools of investment capital; and the more dispersed purchasing power of the middle classes provides a ready market for each new item of conspicuous consumption invented by ingenious industry, whether it be front-loading washing machines or annually restyled automobiles. It is clearly more dynamic to have one's industry geared to instantly obsolete luxuries for the affluent than to the continuing necessities of a non-lucrative population.

Although redistribution of wealth would decrease the rate of total national economic growth, by reducing levels of consumer demand and concentrations of capital in the hands of entrepreneurial and investing classes, the living standards of those who are at present most in need would rise in absolute terms. Because of reduced output there would be diminished per capita demands on the resource base, and conservation would be encouraged. The decision to accept this option would in itself represent a turn away from materialism and conspicuous consumption, and towards organic values and humanism. There are already signs that such an attitude is growing among young people in developed nations, who are joining conservation and voluntary social-work groups in large numbers.[7] Their idealism and their intuitive understanding of what is of lasting value in life will be thwarted if some form of control is not exerted on technological innovation irrespective of its impact on the redistribution of wealth or on the well-being of our common resource base.

A recent suggestion of how this might be done for Britain, in the Rothschild Report on the financing of scientific research, has resulted in widespread criticism by scientists and research workers, who see their independence of action being destroyed.[8] Rothschild suggested that the allocation of government funds for these purposes should be removed from the hands of science research councils, run by eminent scientists themselves, and given to the particular government departments concerned with these matters. In cases such as this, where society as a whole is both the investor and the consumer, this seems to be an admirable approach, bringing the processes of research and development under increasing public scrutiny and control. The principle of power without responsibility can never be a good one, particularly where so much is at stake. The institution of such a system would not of itself bring back runaway technology under social control, but it would make such a development more feasible. As Anthony Tucker, science correspondent of *The Guardian* has pointed out, what is required is research into such subjects as human perception, housing needs, plant-insect relationships, husbandry and sewage processing 'that would stop us chucking £50 million of valuable organic fertilizers into the rivers and seas each year', instead of research into motor-car technology, construction techniques for empty office blocks, and new chemical fertilisers.[9] Concentration on simple processes of meeting fundamental human needs could be linked with the development of 'intermediate technologies', advocated by Schumacher and Illich, producing basic agricultural equipment and machine tools for developing countries.[10] Linked to redistribution of wealth, and increases of funds devoted to public services, such policies could help to narrow the widening gaps of income, life-style and culture between classes and nations in the modern world.

Changing Aspirations

Once established, technical innovations exert far-reaching influences on the nature and quality of human life; indeed this is one of the reasons why it is important to be selective in our attitude to them. Because of the dynamic relationship between values and technology, both are constantly changing. As formal education and individualistic thinking spread throughout the modern world, increasing numbers of people seek to improve their material conditions by using more efficient techniques of production. Developing communications improve knowledge of alternative ways of working and living, and new priorities, distinct from the traditional ones of survival, shelter, nurture, and social acceptability, are making themselves felt. The satisfaction of values such as freedom, choice, leisure, knowledge and glamour, previously confined to small elites, is now being demanded by increasing numbers of ordinary people. Anyone who now states categorically that he knows what large numbers of other people want is risking ridicule.

The dramatic effect of technology on life-styles in the Western World has been evident even within the last 25 years. Domestic appliances and birth-control techniques have freed the housewife from her former daily routine of housework and child-minding; she is now free to take paid employment in the day, and to leave her husband at home baby-sitting while she goes out in the evening to study classes or to play bingo. The division of roles between the sexes is becoming blurred, and neither men nor women have fully come to terms with the new situation. The rapid increase in personal mobility has exerted equally potent influences. People look farther afield for all their activities, and the vitality of local communities is threatened. This is accentuated by the increasing frequency with which people move house—over half the families in England and Wales made at least one move in the 1950s.[11] It would be naive to assume that these changes in life-style are solely responsible for trends such as increase in divorce rates, the mounting tide of couples seeking guidance from marriage counsellors, and the growing problems of loneliness, alienation, and mental stress. Nevertheless such failures of our materially progressive society do indicate an inability to adapt to the fierce rate of technological change to which it is being subjected. The solution is likely to lie in a sensitive selection of which changes will be beneficial, and a prediction of the influences they will have on our lives.

Consumption and Destruction

We have not so far made specific references to one of the most obvious effects of the uncontrolled technical developments of the last two centuries—the despoliation and contamination of large stretches of the earth's surface. By increasing his power to process large volumes of resources for his own use, man has placed himself outside the restraints which operate on all other species, preventing them from doing irreversible damage to the environment. The biblical prophesy 'I said "Ye are gods"' has come true. We are in total control of the world, and recognition of the fact and the responsibilities that it entails should guide our use of technology in the future. The use of resources does not necessarily involve leaving behind the kind of wilderness that we associate with coal-spoil tips, polluted rivers, oil slicks and poisoned food-chains. It is again a question of priorities: maximum production at minimum cost will have this effect, but it is possible to conserve resources by recycling used materials, such as water, steel scrap and pulverised fly ash, rather than leaving them in deadly dumps. The comment that short-term costs would be higher ignores the fact that in the medium and long term the vital resources of life—air, water and soil—must be preserved at whatever cost.

Mines, cities, factories, and power systems use materials and fossil fuels whose extraction, concentration and waste disposal at present rupture the delicate balance of nature, and cause chain reactions of deterioration. The notorious and widely publicised results of the indiscriminate use of DDT have already been referred to; its accumulation in soils, rivers and lakes, and subsequently in the food-chain of animals and human beings,

P.A.H.N.—C

was caused by the fact that it was non-degradable and was used in excessive quantities. Since its further use was banned in the USA, technologists and scientists working for the big chemical companies have announced the development of techniques for coating DDT grains with zinc, and thus rendering them degradable.[12] They had not before addressed themselves to the problem.

The long-term problem of the misuse of the most precious scarce resource of all—water—is even more serious. Throughout the industrialised world it is trapped, piped, used, contaminated and returned in varying states of pollution into rivers or the sea, thus poisoning their organic life, and making them incapable of providing further supplies of water in their lower courses. This deficiency can only be made good at the moment by constructing further reservoirs, or coastal barrages, to collect and contaminate yet more water for domestic and industrial use, until even the rich biological action of the seas is unable to break down the concentrations of chemicals, which damage marine life, and become absorbed into the hydrological cycle, accumulating as an inexorable burden which could eventually exert profound and probably harmful effects on all life, including that of mankind.[13] Less insidious but more dramatic dangers are posed by such developments as the use of nuclear power, with its deadly capacity for gamma radiation from used and dumped uranium, and obsolete power stations; and the stripping of trees, and subsequent gullying and sheet erosion, and the final removal of most organic life from such 'cutover lands' as the western Great Lakes and the Mallee Scrub of southeast Australia. The biosphere (the thin film at the surface of the earth where the conditions necessary for life as we know it exist) could and, indeed, would be rendered temporarily uninhabitable if present rates of pollution per person were to continue for the next several centuries.

Confronted with the far-reaching impact of technological innovations upon aspirations, life-styles, resource potential, and the environment, modern society is constantly trying to adjust to a situation whose accelerating momentum leaves it far behind. Each new development quickly becomes embedded in our social and economic systems, in a way that allows it to give rise to further innovations, and makes it extremely hard to eradicate or control. The motor car is one particularly dominating example, together with its associated phenomena, the caravan, the touring holiday, the motorway and the out-of-town shopping centre. The process of social digestion does not have time to operate before being confronted by a fresh innovation, in this case the 'advanced passenger train', electrically propelled, and possibly hover vehicles, all having very different implications for settlements and society. In summary, all the elements of the planning process are undergoing rapid change: minority values are spreading to increasingly large groups, ranges of choice are being dramatically widened, material conditions are in a state of rapid revolution, and the technology at our disposal is outstripping our capacity to utilise it. There is no longer time for the traditional subconscious techniques of planning, with their heavy reliance on trial and error. Since the old adjustment mechanisms can no longer operate, we must plan in advance.

This cannot be achieved by trying to guess where technology will lead us, and attempting to change society to suit that trend; there must be thoroughgoing insistence on directing it to mirror our changing priorities, and to preserve our irreplaceable resources. Specialisation itself, which lies at the root of civilisation, must be restricted to its proper economic sphere, and not allowed to determine our forms of social organisation, and access to the good things of life.

3 Planning and the Power Structure

Much stress has been placed on the role of planning to rectify the dangerous inequalities of wealth and opportunity which are produced by our competitive economic and social systems. The question arises: 'Is not planning firmly in the hands of those who are benefiting most from this inequality, and is it likely that they will tolerate plans that will decrease their advantages?' The existence of such an 'establishment' or 'power elite' has been indicated by work done by Mills in the USA and Sampson in Britain.[1] When people without power try to get plans of their own accepted, they tend to founder on the opposition of the established authorities, or the individual plan-makers are themselves drawn into the ranks of the elite, and begin to share their attitudes. Are the theory and the practice destined to continue along such separate paths? There are too many examples of 'dynamic conservatism' at work in planning machinery throughout the industrialised world, energetically excluding objections and pursuing the narrow interests of power elites, for us to be optimistic that without intervention the problem will in time solve itself.[2]

The Theory of Intervention
Ideas of participatory democracy have consistently run far ahead

of implementation in modern times. Although social theory has made the long journey from Machiavelli to Mill and the modern pluralists, it is often divorced from any real changes in society, and is used instead as a polite fiction to legitimise the status quo. Any progress in this field must involve some form of confrontation between the grand theory and the reality of unequal opportunities, relative deprivation, and individual alienation.

The results of such inconsistencies are there for all to see, and the physical planner, with his acknowledged responsibility for advising on the location and distribution of activities and services, can hardly do his job without calling attention to the concentrations of poverty, bad housing, and social malaise which stem from them. He also has a professional need to identify the social objectives towards which his plans should work. For him the choice lies between the classical egalitarian view of the greatest happiness for the greatest number, and the partially submerged but largely operational views that 'what is good for General Motors is good for the USA' and what is good for the motor industry is good for the motor worker.

Answers to many of the most crucial questions about the correct relations between a society and its planning can be found in the distinguished mainstream of British social philosophy; these include the circumstances in which government intervention in the affairs of the individual may be justified, the rights of minority groups, and the problems of conflict between consensus and individual values. Even Locke's concept of the social contract has some significance for these issues, implying that certain sacrifices of personal liberty must be made in order to achieve the advantages of living in a safe and ordered society. By the time of Jeremy Bentham, the Utilitarians were asking more pointed questions about what should be the aims of society and the role of government. The approach adopted to these issues by John Stuart Mill is of particular interest to both politics and planning.[3] He divided human activities into those that are primarily 'self-affecting', and should not be the subject of external regulation, and others that are primarily 'other affecting' and should be so regulated.[4]

Thus the conditions under which a man is employed, the distribution of wealth, the provision of decent housing and social services are all clearly 'other-affecting' because the conduct of individuals in these fields will directly affect large numbers of other people very intimately. They are, therefore, the proper concern of democratically elected governments. Failure to debate, legislate, and implement policies on these matters is to betray the social contract, and will lead on to exploitation of the weak by the relatively stronger.

On the other hand there are a number of issues whose significance is largely personal and which should not be the subject of social interference: these include religion, freedom of opinion and speech, sexual but not social morality, personal expenditure and choice of value systems. Mill himself was very conscious of the irony that at the time of his writing the state interfered in precisely those matters in which it should not, concerning individual beliefs and life-styles, and failed to intervene where it should in matters of social welfare.

Although the victims of Victorian laissez-faire were the toiling *masses,* situations can arise where they are disadvantaged *minorities,* whose exploitation is made possible by the neutrality or the active support of a complacent majority, as is the case with American Indians, Australian aborigines, British immigrants, one-parent families, unemployed and unskilled workers, and itinerants such as gypsies. The planning machinery must ensure equality for such groups in social opportunities, but must avoid interference in their personal lives.

It is also important to recognise the essential diversity of interests of individuals, groups and classes. The naive assumtion of the positivists that a small elite could know what was best for the whole of society is particularly beguiling to many radicals, reformers and utopians, but it implies the worst kind of authoritarianism. As Mill pointed out, diversity of opinion should be encouraged, not only because today's error may be tomorrow's truth, or because error can only be established as such by being examined, but also because without its challenge there will be no stimulating force to keep truth vital and ensure its progressive enlargement.[5] Such a view allows us to discard authoritarian notions about discovering and implementing consensus views of the general good, irrespective of the actual preferences of individuals and groups. It also suggests a means of approaching consultation, and alerts us to the likely way in which pressures will be brought to bear by particular groups. A road-transport organisation, such as the British Road Federation, for example, may mobilise its considerable resources to campaign for the construction of more urban motorways, and generate an impression of immense popular support for them, while the many thousands of people who will be intimately affected by the resulting demolitions, dislocation and pollution may find it much more difficult to make their views heard.[6]

If the license of one group is not to become the burden of others, it must be recognised that often the worst case is put most noisily. Only by constant inquiry, analysis and redefinition of issues can a middle course be steered, avoiding both the pretentions of the bigot to legislate for the 'moral welfare' of his fellow citizens and the claims of the profit-seeking businessman to freedom from proper social constraints over his activities. Any government interference should be demonstrably in the interests of those most acutely affected, and this can only be achieved by consultation before decisions are made, and participation in the way they are implemented and reviewed.

The problem, in the words of Keith Jackson of Liverpool University, is that 'We are democratic in general political principle, but paternalist and elitist in particular practical cases'.[7] This contradiction can be overcome at two stages – that of planning and that of management. Residents' groups can be contacted, people's aspirations and priorities surveyed, and public discussions stimulated, before the first stages of development of proposals are started by the planners. The other problem, that of incorporating local people into the running of their own services, is largely outside the scope of this book, but it should be said that there is no reason why, for instance, council tenants' associations should not share control over open spaces and communal facilities within their estates jointly with corporation officials, or why residents' associations should not be given control over the local environment in their own areas. The argument of New York's Mayor Lindsay that the time has come for a sharing of power back from the centre to the locality is surely right.[8]

The Reality of Manipulation

The present pattern is for established authority, having decided that a certain policy is in the public interest (or, more cynically, in its own), to set about winning the compliance of the rest of the community by public-relations exercises in the press and on radio and television. The massive redevelopment of the centres of cities like Boston and Philadelphia, which primarily benefits the consortia of businessmen entrusted with its execution, and which deprives thousands of poor families of cheap and convenient homes, is publicised in glossy brochures and even glossier film strips as 'the way in which the city is preparing to meet the challenge of the future'.[9] Protest is ignored by the city business and political machines, which know that under the present set-up no one can stop them doing what they want. Professor Nathan Glazer has written of this process:

> The urban-renewal agency does in fact represent a current threat to many: destroying small businessmen, evicting older people from their tenements, forcing families from their homes, *and then failing to relocate them in decent, safe, sanitary, and reasonably priced housing as required by law* [author's italics]. It is apparent that the urban-renewal agency is a more vivid threat to security than the banker, in these days of amortized mortgages.[10]

This problem created by the urban financial and political establishment, activated purely by its own interests, misusing the machinery originally intended to benefit the underprivileged residents of inner-city areas, forms an underlying theme of Jane Jacobs' book *The Death and Life of American Cities*; it also highlights the ways that city administrations, universities and business consortia enter into unholy trinities to dispossess the people of whole areas by compulsory acquisition of their homes (under compulsory purchase powers or 'eminent domain') and replace them with vast educational and commercial complexes, protected from invasion by city residents with barbed wire and Alsatian guard dogs.[11] Planners involved in such schemes rely on naked power for their support as much as did the builders of the pyramids or the bailiffs of feudal landlords. Every kind of sleight of hand is used, including condemning sound buildings as slums when their sites are required for a profitable redevelopment scheme, and rating alternative accommodation occupied by displaced families as satisfactory when it is not.[12] If we look for the objectives underlying these schemes, they emerge as private profit for the businessmen, increased rateable value from the central area for the city government and professional satisfaction for the urban planner, who has moved his city closer to the inhuman ideal of Le Corbusier's Radiant City. What we do *not* find is any concern for the objectives of the residents or users of the areas.

We have already mentioned the similar case of British city-centre shopping precincts. As British towns approach saturation point for such indigestible features, they are being succeeded by even more costly and unnecessary 'Civic Centres'. In Liverpool, where the city is too impoverished to equip its new public housing estates on the edge of the city with basic social, recreational and shopping facilities, a new 'Civic Centre' is being planned to house corporation officials in the very heart of the city at a cost of £17 million[13]—though there is ample unused office accommodation throughout the city to provide for any extra requirements that the corporation might have. Aesthetically the scheme is so bad that the City Planning Department opposes it, and the Royal Fine Art Commission says that it would destroy the existing character of the town centre while contributing nothing original: 'A decision to allocate funds to one particular project such as the civic centre or the new road system could mean that the council is condemning old people to live for a further number of years in squalid conditions'.[14]

There is a real danger that the wide powers of compulsory acquisition of land and buildings conferred on planners by politicians in the name of social justice and public welfare will be used by the power elite to pursue their own narrow interests to the detriment of those very groups whose problems should be planners' first concern—the underprivileged, under-serviced, underconsulted, underskilled and impoverished groups who represent the failure of affluent societies to distribute their wealth and power equitably.

Community Action

Individuals and groups outside the power structure have attempted to plan for their own welfare since the beginning of recorded history. Both Abraham and Moses and their followers are early examples, and both were remarkably successful, relying as much on their ability to put physical space between themselves and their oppressors as on divine intervention. The English Diggers are another particularly interesting example. An egalitarian group of Parliamentary soldiers who at the end of the Civil War in 1649 occupied Clapham Common near London, and set about establishing there a communal and fraternal farming community, they were imprisoned by the army, their homes burned, and their crops trampled.[15]

Thus the first recorded example of the squatting movement in Britain was put down, not to reappear for over a century, in starkly contrasting circumstances and with equally contrasting success. This time the members of the elite did the squatting, in the Enclosure Movement of the late eighteenth century and early nineteenth, by which tens of thousands of acres of common land, traditionally the common property of the local villagers, were seized by local landowners and occupied without compensation. This was legitimised by the passage of hundreds of Enclosure Acts through parliament. The loss of this pasture land fatally damaged the agricultural economy of thousands of villages, and drove tides of impoverished families to seek work in the growing industrial towns, where the landowners invested their capital.[16] Both the Diggers and the Enclosure Act landlords were engaging in intelligent and self-conscious attempts at planning to use resources in their own interests. Those who were inside the power structure succeeded; those outside failed and were punished.

Nevertheless, Robert Owen re-establishd the fact that alternative plans could be successfully implemented, within the structure of existing society, with his model industrial settlement of New Lanark, of which he was first manager and then proprietor from 1800 to 1825.[17] New Lanark achieved the economic and social success that Owen had predicted, the workers being housed in a model village of high quality built beside the River Clyde, and working similar hours to those of today; education was provided for children, and the whole scheme produced a handsome profit. Despite the failure of Owen's later experiment of 'New Harmony' in Indiana, USA, many of the model towns of the nineteenth century, the growth of trade unions, and the cooperative movement owed much to his teachings, and his work lives on in them to the present.

Probably the most highly publicised modern expression of Owen's ideas are the Hippies who seek to establish their alternative society by physically escaping from the urban scene of a middle-aged, middle-class and materialist culture. In their determination to 'do their own thing' the Hippy Communes have something in common with the militant syndicalists and guild socialists, with their slogan of 'Don't Protest—Occupy'. Organisations who help people to squat in vacant houses, or take over unused office blocks, are opposing their own plans to those of the power structure, and they are frequently successful in making bureaucrats acknowledge their responsibility to alleviate problems of homelessness and overcrowding.[18] Many 'squatters' in Britain in the past 3 years have been confirmed in their tenancies. Others have been rehoused in suitable accommodation by the local council which had previously denied it could do anything to help them.[19] These victories are small-scale and isolated, but nonetheless significant in illustrating the way that the planning of the power structure can be challenged by direct action, contrasting the theory of a decent home for everyone with the reality of homelessness.

More significant still, and on a far wider scale, are the rapidly increasing numbers of Tenants' and Residents' Associations, and Neighbourhood and Community Councils, which are demanding information from planners about proposals affecting their localities. Not only are they criticising existing proposals and past mistakes, they are also insisting on consultation and partnership in the development of future plans. Their right to participate was officially acknowledged in the terms of reference of the Skeffington Committee on Public Participation in Planning.[20] One of the recommendations made by the Committee was that Local Planning Authorities should attempt to stimulate bodies, which it termed 'Community Forums', to express the objectives of local people. Shorn of its quaint associations with classical Rome, this concept differs little from that of the Residents' Association, membership of which is open to all who live in the area.[21]

The exhortation of the Skeffington Report to consult is supported by the statutory requirement of the 1968 Town and Country Planning Act to do so, though the ways in which this should be done are left so ill defined that a great deal of discretion remains with the individual planning authority.[22] Nonetheless, Residents' and Tenants' Associations are increasingly conscious of their right to be heard, and they are rapidly acquiring mastery over the planning procedures and jargon which represent the undigested accretions of 25 years of bureaucratic control. The case of Liverpool's Amalgamated Tenants' Association Coordinating Committee (ATACC) exemplifies this new self-confidence and effectiveness. Following a rent rise in council houses in 1967 and a rash of complaints about maintenance and bad design, there was a series of rent strikes throughout the corporation's estates. Tenants' Associations grew rapidly, and the housing department decided that discussions were necessary; these proved so fruitful in identifying causes of discontent, and the means of rectifying them, that they were continued on a monthly basis. Each monthly meeting was attended by a representative from each Tenants' Association, senior officers from a number of other corporation departments (as well as from housing), and councillors serving on the appropriate committees.[23]

Community Organisations

Community organisations of many different types are springing up throughout Britain and America. Many tend to be informal in their structure, and have grown out of strong local feeling on one or more particular issues, such as the threat of slum clearance, 'gentrification' or unpopular road proposals. Increasingly, however, they are beginning to assume some permanence, and to become recognised as legitimate voices of local opinion. In London the Notting Hill Residents' Association has survived and grown for over a decade; and in Newcastle the West End Tenants' Association is still strong after 7 years of existence, as is Liverpool's Kensington and Anfield Community Association (KAFCA), which is of a similar age.

Two particularly interesting suggestions for future development are those of Liverpool's Neighbourhood Organisation Committee and the Institute of Community Studies' Neighbourhood Council Movement. The former is a loose federation of the city's eighty-odd local groups into a forum for discussion of issues of common interest, which local authority chief officers may be asked to attend to give information. The structures of the local groups and the Neighbourhood Organisation Committee itself are very loosely defined, a situation which is sometimes justified on the ground that it keeps them clear of party political domination, maintains their flexibility and sensitivity to local needs, and favours informal links with corporation officials. The establishment of a system of fully elected Neighbourhood Councils, each with an electorate of about 10,000 persons, would, by contrast, rest on a much more formal basis. Such an approach is recommended by Michael Young of the Institute of Community Studies.[24]

The first application of such ideas in an urban area is taking place in the Golborne Ward of North Kensington in London, a district with a long record of social stress and conflict, where George Clark, a social activist, helped to establish a Residents' Association in the early 1960s. In April 1971 elections were held under the supervision of an independent body to form a

Neighbourhood Council. Within a year the Council had achieved two major successes. The Greater London Council was persuaded to buy properties on which intolerable noise levels had been inflicted as a result of the opening of a very long stretch of elevated motorway (the notorious 'Westway'), and to offer those displaced the alternative of moving into council housing.[25] Even more significantly, the Neighbourhood Council has been taken into partnership by the Greater London Council in the redevelopment of the large Swinbrook area, involving 1,400 dwellings. In February 1972 the Chairman of the GLC's Housing Committee announced that he would ask the Council to back a scheme that would involve the full participation of the slum dwellers themselves.[26] Only a third of the Steering Committee is to come from the Greater London Council; a third will come from the Royal Borough of Kensington, and the remaining third will be drawn directly from the community and such organisations as the Neighbourhood Council. In the USA a third approach has been pioneered in the Community Action Projects of the Office of Equal Opportunity, where local steering committees are elected specifically to participate in the running of particular projects.[27] Since the OEO is committed to a local grass-roots approach, results have varied sharply between different schemes, but there has been a tendency for local people to be manipulated or subjected to 'talk therapy' by the officials involved.[28] The Community Demonstration Agencies of the Model Cities Programme and the Community Action Projects of OEO have made large sums available to grass-roots local organisations, and in Philadelphia the Area Wide Council (a federation of neighbourhood organisations) was granted more than $20,000 a month to employ its own technicians and run its own organisation.[29] In general, citizen participation has been taken further, and achieved more, in the USA than anywhere else, but it is by no means certain that the best method of organisation has yet been achieved.

It is certainly too early to be dogmatic about which approach will prove to be the most fruitful. Each shares a common insistence on consultation with local people, and each is developing its own ways of achieving participation in the making of decisions. The 'organic' approach being adopted in Liverpool lacks accountability but gains through being acceptable to established bodies, such as corporation departments. The use of citizen committees to cooperate in running community projects on the American model is logical, and in theory democratic, but is prone to manipulation. The election of continuing Neighbourhood Councils is effective and democratic, but runs the twin risks of either being absorbed into the existing party political power structures, thus losing its truly local flavour, or failing for lack of interest. Experiments of all three types—and possibly the invention of new variations—should all be welcomed. It is clear that in all its various forms the movement is growing rapidly, and will have enormous significance for physical planning.

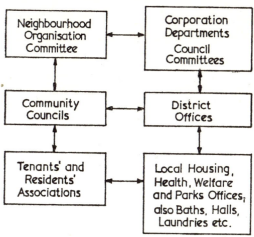

Fig 1 Consultation and Participation Structure for Liverpool

If planners really do want to discover the grain of local community life, and the human and social priorities of the people for whom they are planning, the neighbourhood organisation, whether elective or not, presents a natural way into the activity. It will provide a meeting place, an organisation capable of contacting other residents, and a channel for collecting and distributing information. But consultation with Residents' Associations should not be treated as a cheap alternative to carrying out attitudes and priorities surveys of people in areas where action is proposed, but rather as a means of ensuring that such a survey gets well informed answers because people will have been stimulated to discuss the issues.

Fig 1 shows how this 'alternative' community structure might relate to corporation departments.

Ultimately there is no reason why a considerable number of the present functions of local councils should not be administered by local groups; for instance, the control of the Parks and Gardens Department over the physical environment of council estates should be left to the local Tenants' Association, which will know much more about the needs, problems, and available spaces than anyone else. Likewise community and recreational facilities such as halls and swimming baths should be planned and run jointly with local bodies.

Who Are the Planners?

Firstly, they are strongly identified with government, over 70 per cent of chartered British planners being directly employed by central or local government, and thus subject to strong pressure to conform to established policy.[30] At the same time, their position inside the power structure does allow individual planners to influence the development of new policies both by research and informed comment. In contrast, there are few contacts between British planners and the business world, for whose interests they tend to have less than average sympathy (50 per cent of the respondents to a 1968 survey favoured the Labour and Liberal parties, as against 43 per cent nationally, while only 29 per cent favoured the Conservatives, traditionally the party of big business, as against 51 per cent nationally).[31]

The option which British planners have of being closely allied and sympathetic to government but generally hostile to business is not open to American planners. In the USA there is a less marked separation of political and financial power (as Mills showed in his work on the Power Elite), so that government and business often have indistinguishable interests.[32] Land use planning is not so securely entrenched within the administrative system as in Britain, nor do government employees have the same security of employment. Many more planners are employed by research and development corporations like Arthur D. Little & Associates, which rely for much of their incomes on business concerns, while a high proportion of the most talented join business-sponsored bodies like the Rand Corporation. Even in the universities a high proportion of funds comes from business contracts and grants.[33]

In Britain, and other West European countries with mixed economies like Sweden, Denmark, Austria and the Netherlands, it is possible for government to see its aims as being distinct from those of organised business, so that the planner's position as a public employee does not necessarily place him in a servile position to the central business complex. Firms may be (and are) refused permission to develop where they wish on the grounds that the employment they could provide is more needed elsewhere. During the discussions of the late 1960s on the reorganisation of local government, central government planners pressed for a city region basis that would have favoured the most underprivileged at the expense of the more affluent, and when their proposals were overturned by the incoming Conservative government they publicised their opposition.

Of course this opposition does not obscure the fact that in this instance a planning decision is being taken in the interests of the power elite against the advice of professionals. Had the general election of June 1970 been held 3 months later, however, the opposite result would have been achieved, as the necessary legislation was already prepared and awaiting debate in that session. Thus in Britain planners are confronted by one party representing the interests of business, which fewer than half of them support; while in the USA *both* parties are inextricably committed to business, without whose financial support no presidential candidate could hope to be elected.

As a result, British planners do have (within the limits of the 'dynamic conservatism' of government departments) much greater scope for analysis and action. They have a legislative mandate to tackle specific social problems, such as bad housing and environmental pollution; considerable legal powers to control the actions of industry and investors; a growing consumer movement to balance against the demands of business; and the constant curiosity of a diverse mass media, parts of which are truly independent, into the unequal distribution of benefits throughout society. By temperament many of them are likely to welcome this room for manoeuvre.[34]

The question remains, however, whether planners are educationally and intellectually equipped to understand and interpret the problems of the world outside their offices. Both in the USA and Britain a significant change is taking place in the composition of the profession. Domination by other professionals (especially engineers, surveyors, and architects) interested in particular aspects of the physical environment is giving place to a situation where planning offices are staffed by well balanced teams of largely graduate planners, many having first qualifications in such coherent disciplines as geography, economics, philosophy and sociology. As the first wave of prewar transplanted professionals age and retire, they are being replaced by people with a greater self-consciousness and awareness of their social role. Many have had the advantage of higher education, when for a number of years they were encouraged to ask the question 'Why?' Because he is able to ask this question, and not just the 'How?' of his predecessors, the modern planner is in a far better position to criticise and reformulate accepted government policy.

The recent development of advocacy planning in both Britain and the USA is an expression of this new and healthy trend. Activists like Paul and Linda Davidoff, whose 'Suburban Action' is trying to blast open American suburbs to accommodate large numbers of the poor black and overcrowded populace of urban ghettos, and Ken Coates, seeking to organise residents in a slum district of Nottingham to articulate their priorities for the area as against those of the city council, are both planners and dissident intellectuals at the same time.[36, 35] The profession is becoming further radicalised because many planners who wish to carry out advocacy work or develop new theories of social action become academics, and through their teaching stimulate new generations of activists.

Unless it is challenged by powerful federations of citizens' groups, ultimate power will continue to rest in the hands of established authority. Nevertheless, there are signs of a new and significant independence of mind among young professional planners, and an awareness that it is possible for them to create their own constituencies by going direct to the groups of people most likely to be affected by planning proposals, and using *their* objectives as the basis of future plans for their areas.[37] We have seen that in both the USA and Britain there is a rapid growth taking place in the number and power of community associations and neighbourhood councils, which could provide the local half of an alliance of dissident intellectuals and community activists. There is nothing inevitable about the sacrifice of the interests of poor and fragmented groups to those of rich and successful ones; it is the result of good organisation, determination and acquisition of knowledge, and it can be countered by the same means.

Planners are neither paid nor employed by small coteries, party caucuses, or particular classes, but by governments responsible to the whole community. Since it is part of their job to see that future demands can be met in socially acceptable ways, there is every reason that they should engage in a maximum of continuous contact with local groups throughout the city, not merely relaying information, but learning about local problems and priorities.

4 *What Values?*
Whose Objectives?

In its simplest terms physical planning is an attempt to satisfy human and social aims by providing appropriate and well placed buildings and facilities. Thus a desire for improvements in health should give rise to conveniently located hospitals, clinics, or a new system of organised home-care. This concept has a seductive simplicity which has led astray many enthusiasts who have used their intuition first to sense society's objectives, and then to dream up total new environments, like Le Corbusier's 'City for Three Million Inhabitants' and 'City of Tomorrow'.[1] Such an approach may be admirable when it is used by thinkers like More and Mannheim to indicate the ultimate directions in which we should be moving. [2, 3] But as a method of planning towns for the people of today it is desperately deficient. What should be a contribution to society's most vital discussion—how the values of its members can best be satisfied—becomes an authoritarian substitute to debate.

The failings of intuitive planning are twofold. First, even the greatest and most humane thinker cannot accurately sense the precise problems and priorities of his fellow citizens. Second, the conviction that there is only one particular *way* of satisfying these wants is unlikely to be right.

In contemporary Western societies there is an impressive array of ways of discovering objectives. There is an advanced educational system, freedom of speech, a developed technology of communication, and a formal democratic structure. Local voluntary bodies are eager to represent their members' views of local priorities. Promotional and pressure groups exist largely for precisely this purpose. Whole cities can be, and have been, polled. People who will be affected by proposed action can be informed and consulted so that their preferences *can* form the basis of the final design, since, although not everyone will want the same things, it is possible and desirable to plan for diversity. But politicians who are responsible to the electorate rightly regard ultimate decisions on objectives as being their concern. Does this mean that all other forms of consultation are superfluous, or even anti-democratic?

If it is to avoid becoming an alternative autocracy, planning must take place inside a political context; politicians must play a major role in deciding on strategic planning objectives. To do this well, they must be supplied with as much relevant information as possible. This applies as much to planning as to finance, defence, foreign policy, internal affairs, or health; but one of the planning matters on which they need to be informed is the pattern of priorities of people who will be affected by development proposals. It is neither practicable nor desirable for the final decision to be removed from their hands. They have the control of the funds which must be allocated to implement proposals, and they are subject to re-election or replacement by the electorate in a way that gives them a direct social mandate that planners can only claim at secondhand. The real question is not whether to consult politicians or the people who will be affected, but whether politicians possess such an accurate knowledge of local and urban objectives that it is superfluous to supply them with extra information.

There are two main reasons why this is not so; local councillors are not perfectly representative of the areas for which they are elected; and it is not practicable for them to spend large amounts of time discovering the individual priorities of the electorate. In Britain and the USA they are elected by a minority of the eligible voters; in Britain in 1967, fewer than a fifth of the population had *ever* got in touch with a local councillor.[4] Party politics dominate city council elections, and in Britain there is a strong tendency for local elections to be used as a means of protest against the political party in power nationally. Local politicians are elected by a small minority on the basis of their adherence to one of two or three very general political philosophies rather than as representatives of specific local viewpoints. The fact that they are delegates selected to take strategic decisions, and not pure representatives deputed to pursue local priorities, is not necessarily a criticism of the existing system. It does nevertheless invalidate the argument that the representation of detailed local priorities is one of their primary roles, and should be entirely left to them.

It is sometimes argued that councillors are so inherently part of their local communities that they will instinctively know what local people will want, but this is not certain. Recent studies have shown that because the local councillors' job is unpaid and part time, they tend to be older, wealthier, and in better jobs than the people they represent.[5] Only 12 per cent of councillors are women, though a large part of a council's work is concerned with family and social problems. Over a fifth are retired, more than half aged over fifty-five, and less than a quarter aged forty-five or less. Employers, managers and professional people constitute three times the proportion of councillors than they do of the general population, and skilled workers and manual labourers are drastically underrepresented.

Even assuming that it was the job of the councillor simply to act as a posting box for the priorities of his ward, there are a number of reasons why he cannot. As soon as he takes his seat on the council, he is drafted on to a number of committees having city-wide responsibilities, and is constantly reminded by committee chairmen and council officials that his loyalties must now be to the whole city. In the party caucus also the accusation of paro-

chialism must be avoided by the aspiring politician. The sheer
burden of keeping abreast of reports to committees from different
departments leaves the part-time unpaid councillor little opportunity to do more than attend a weekly or fortnightly 'surgery'
in his own ward, which cannot give him the thorough knowledge
of detail on which planning should be based.[6] This difficulty is
being continuously deepened by the growing size of cities and
the limited number of members that a council may have if it is
to remain an effective decision-taking body. In big cities like
Manchester and Birmingham, wards represented by three councillors have already passed the 20,000 population mark, and
under the reorganisation of local government which will take
place in 1974, wards may in some cases have to double their size,
to become the equivalent in population of small cities. Earnestly
as they may try, councillors will not be able to maintain close
and continuous contact with all sections of such large
communities.

How Planners Can Help the Local Councillor

Many city councillors are among the unsung heroes of modern
British society. Saddled for the last century with a local government structure that has become increasingly anachronistic and
fragmented, at the same time as urban problems have grown in
scale, complexity and severity, they have worked with intelligence
and enthusiasm to administer an increasing range of local
government services, in ways that have not only maintained but
sometimes improved the quality of urban life. Individual councils
have initiated developments in housing, education and care of
the elderly which have set patterns for the rest of Britain, and,
in some cases, further afield.[7] Despite the enormous sums of
money which they are responsible for distributing, cases of cor-
ruption have been rare, although those that have occurred have
fortunately been seized upon by an alert national press.

It is unfortunate that the work of good councillors is often
outweighed both in the public's eyes, and in reality, by the
tendency for party machines to fall into the hands of those more

interested in the wielding of power for its own sake than for the introduction of any particular social improvements. Because the work of local authorities in Britain is conducted in considerable secrecy, and departmental reports are not available to the public, who are also excluded from crucial committee meetings, caucus politics develop rapidly, and it is often the schemer rather than the innovator or the reformer who gains control. A small number of councillors are local businessmen pursuing their sometimes legal, but seldom legitimate, self-interest. Numerically these two groups form a very small minority of all local councillors, but they wield disproportionate power, and attract most public interest. If their role is to be diminished, and the image of local government improved, there must be greater open-ness and discussion about local issues.

If it is accepted that councillors, struggling with the vast problems of the modern city, cannot hope to maintain continuous and intimate contact with the people of their own wards, but that plans for localities should not be prepared without consulting the people who will be most affected, some alternative means of communication must be developed. It is here that the full-time, fully paid planner should help. During the exchange of information, and consultation about options, alternatives, and priorities, the local councillor can be involved; and he can make use of the results to gain a more detailed knowledge of his own area, and to become better known to his electors and a more credible representative figure to them. Consultation between local people and council officials can help to reinvigorate local democracy. A recent example of this, which has already been mentioned in Chapter 3, is the work of Liverpool's Amalgamated Tenants' Associations Coordinating Committee (ATACC), which brings together chairmen or deputy chairmen of council committees, professional officers, and tenants' representatives.[8] It would be wrong to pretend that ATACC has solved all the problems of council housing in Liverpool, but it has helped to improve councillors', officials', and tenants' understanding of each other's problems; its affect has been to strengthen rather than weaken the local democratic process.

The Citizen as Planning Consultant

Tenants' and residents' associations can claim, on several grounds, the right to be consulted about proposals for their localities. They have their roots in the area, and know more acutely than councillors or officials what it is like to be on the receiving end of policy decisions. They are likely to be influential in the community. They will be able and keen to relay both general information from council to local people and detailed accounts of problems and preferences back to corporation officials. If alienated or ignored, they may be able to undermine the success of plans that they may have good reason to dislike. If involved, they may bring real knowledge and insight to bear on local problems. Because their members are by temperament leaders and joiners, and of above average energy and articulateness, they frequently have the capacity to crystallise prevailing attitudes, and to invent original solutions to widespread local problems, with which, unlike the planners, they have to live.

Where such associations exist, they form ideal starting points for consultation, because their members will introduce the issues into the most important debating chambers of all—the corner shop, the coffee trolley, the works canteen, and the local pub. The facts that tenants' and residents' associations are not truly representative of the whole community, are often ephemeral and prone to splits, do not lessen their right to be heard. Clearly the discovery of their objectives is a necessary but not sufficient first step in consultation.

Promotional and pressure groups perform a similar role at the larger scale of city and regional planning. Suspicious as one must be of the vested interests of such pressure groups as the British Road Federation, the American Medical Association and the US firearms lobby, they are part of the political world in which planners operate, and in all likelihood they will continue to be part of the society that will implement the plans. Failure to consult pressure groups would be unrealistic; equally, unquestioning acceptance of the validity of their objectives for the rest of society would be naïve.

Promotional groups, by contrast, often consist of individuals fired by a set of ideals. Ebenezer Howard's and Raymond Unwin's Garden City Movement produced the ideas and raised the funds to establish Letchworth and Welwyn Garden Cities, the first two pioneering new towns of modern times.[9] The Town and Country Planning Association, which grew out of this movement, has for over half a century been enormously influential in identifying the problems of British towns and producing a stream of practical suggestions as to how they should be tackled. With a membership which has never risen above 5,000, they have placed themselves at the head of the successful campaigns for new towns, and against tower blocks. Academics, publicists, journalists, politicians, professionals and inspired amateurs join together in developing and popularising ideas in the association's journal *Town and Country Planning,* and in books and articles.[10] The opinions of such bodies as the TCPA, the New York Regional Plan Association, The Council for the Preservation of Rural England, and the Child Poverty Action Group should be given every attention in the discussion of planning objectives; their views are expert, disinterested, and sufficiently convincing to have won and retained the active involvement of numbers of people without thought of material personal gain.

By contrast, the urban poll, seeking the opinion of the entire electorate, may not be very meaningful, unless it deals with specific single issues and is preceded by programmes of carefully planned public discussion in press, radio and television. Even then, there is the danger that only a small minority will vote, and that they will give the answer that they have been guided to favour. The difficulty is that, while as individuals we are very good at recognising our preferences on issues immediately affecting us, we are far less ready at deciding which of several patterns of land use will best serve our interests. Nevertheless, there have been several interesting initiatives of this sort recently in both Britain and the USA. Los Angeles Planning Department has conducted a poll to see which of four strategies is favoured by the majority of voters in the city, and a similar exercise has been conducted by the South Hampshire Regional Strategy team.[11]

Whether or not the results of such surveys are sufficiently conclusive to form the basis for a planning strategy is arguable. Selecting the shape of a plan before one has decided on the detailed problems seems to be jumping to conclusions. An opposite approach of building up from specific solutions is both more logical, and more sensitive to local conditions and preferences.[12]

A more appropriate use for an urban poll is to discover what relative priority citizens would give to different general objectives such as improved housing, cheaper and more frequent public transport, reduced city rates, or more roads. The resulting ranking would then be composed of a certain number of mentions, with a specific order of importance attached to each. This would be a partial approach to discovering the utilitarian ideal of 'the greatest happiness for the greatest number'. The present writer has employed this method in a number of student projects, with considerable apparent success. Since the recognition of a problem implies the existence of a frustrated objective, and since it is problems which people are most conscious of, we simply asked interviewees to mention the most acute problems in the area which future planning should aim to solve. We then asked them to say which of these seemed to them the most important, the next so, and which others seem very important, thus giving us gradings of four different levels of priority. As a means of deriving ranked objectives for a regional or urban structure plan, this approach deserves consideration. It is a more constructive use of an urban poll than the selection of one of a number of strategies, or, for instance, finding out whether or not to build council houses on a derelict park site.[13] It is being given its first practical (as against academic) application by the joint team, working under Peter Wood, who are preparing a structure plan for the Merseyside conurbation. Having had a successful response from local councillors, they are about to embark on a sample survey of the population at large, which, though statistically reliable, will cost a total of less than £10,000, half of which is being met by a grant from the Department of the Environment.

Desirable as the kind of process discussed above may be, it

is not so urgently imperative as is consultation with people living in 'action areas'—those which are going to be drastically affected by new proposals. At the moment localities are classed as slums and demolished, or termed 'General Improvement Areas', and scheduled for new investment, with a minimum of discussion with the people at present living there about what they would like to be done, or the type of dwelling or neighbourhood in which they would like to be rehoused.[14] The municipal bulldozer moves in, and sweeps through, or by, their homes with no more concern for local preferences than the tank of an invading army. If the state wishes to intervene in the lives of individual families on grounds of health or welfare, then the individual must be given some say in the kind of benefits that will be imposed on him; otherwise he is the victim of the worst kind of paternalist interference.

Contrasting Approaches: London and Paris

The organisation of public meetings, addressed by council members and officials in areas where action is being planned, has long been regarded by planners as a tedious public relations exercise. Such meetings are normally held after policy has been decided, and consist of the platform speakers telling the people what is going to happen in general, and local people from the floor raising angry and particular objections, which can be overruled or accepted without endangering the plan's basic aims. This bland approach was tried in the redevelopment of the area surrounding London's Covent Garden wholesale fruit and flower market. The proposal was to clear and rebuild an area of 96 acres as a modernistic hotel, offices, shopping, luxury housing and conference centre; nearly all the existing population of 3,000 people of very mixed class and income would have been displaced. The original stimulus to the scheme came from the necessary removal of the market to a less central site, but the market only occupies 15 acres, or less than one-sixth of the designated area.[15] Local opposition to the scheme stems from the fact that while both the Greater London Council and the property developers would make enormous profits, local people would be deprived of their homes and workplaces, and London would lose a uniquely quiet, intimate and historic central district.

Participation has been non-existent, and consultation a mockery. The original chairman of the Development Committee wrote to the planner in charge of the scheme advising him that residents' groups were more trouble than they were worth.[16] His successor invited members of the community association to County Hall for a working lunch which has since become fabled for the high quality of the food and service, and the lack of any useful discussion. At about this time it became apparent that very few of the existing residents would be able to afford the rents that would be charged in the new development; Brian Anson and Art Muscovitch, two senior members of the planning team, resigned and joined the Community Association. In an effort to appease local indignation a public relations document was produced entitled *Look at the Facts,* which stated: 'You can make sure that you will be heard by contacting the development team. They have the facts and figures'. Such an approach is no more than the use of statistics to beat local people over the head with.

Although only 3,000 people live in the area, the Community has a mailing list of over 4,000, and its activities have aroused national interest and sympathy. The issue was that powers that were intended to be used to improve living conditions for the underpriviledged were being employed as a steamroller in the interests of enormous profits. Developers, planners and politicians decided that new hotels and conference facilities were necessary and that Covent Garden was the most lucrative site for them. If alternative sites had been considered, nobody had been told. The community, by insisting that its rights be taken into account, brought the discussion back on to a realistic human level. As the editor of their newspaper observed: 'The people here simply do not want big hotels and a conference hall or car parking for 2,000. Only 200 of them own cars.'[17]

After 2 years of conflict the Secretary of State for the Environment decided to uphold many of the objectors' points. In particular he rejected the need for an enormous increase in hotel and shopping space, and stressed the need for conservation of character and scale. He also refused to sanction the road proposals that would have formed the first piece of a jigsaw puzzle of inner area urban motorways.[18]

In retrospect, the two major issues to emerge are whether planning powers can legitimately be used as a means of acquiring extensive tracts of land in private possession to create attractively large and continuous sites for property developers to clear and redevelop at enormous profit; and, quite separately, whether there may sometimes be irreconcilable conflicts between the interests of localities and those of the wider city. On the first issue there seems little doubt that the driving out of unwilling residents to create extra wealth for property companies is a prostitution of planning—a view that was presumably shared by the two GLC planners who resigned over this issue.

On the second point there are a number of ways of avoiding or resolving genuine conflicts, one of which has been used by the Council of Paris in planning the development of an area very similar to Covent Garden— the old wholesale meat and fruit market of Les Halles in Montorgueil, after its function had been transferred to Rungis in 1967. They notified the 3,000 local residents and business people that the area was to be redeveloped, and of the essential urban functions that they wanted to locate there, including the construction of a section of the new express metro, and a public library with space for a million books and 1,300 readers. The residents then organised themselves into a Union of Residents' Associations for the planning of the centres of St Martins and neighbourhood, and employed two architects and a town planner, who drew up a scheme for the restoration of the area, accommodating the new developments but also including shops, offices, green spaces, clinic, crèches, and preserving some existing dwellings. The council broadly approved the plan, and delegated its development control powers in the area to the Union of Residents' Associations. The benefits have been very real. Local control has ensured that short-term use of doomed buildings has been promoted, and small boutiques and crafts-men's shops have mushroomed in the area, taking advantage of low rent short-term leases. Local people identify with the plan, instead of doing all they can to obstruct it, as in London. Most important of all, there will be continuity of people, activity, and atmosphere.

Consultation—a Modest Proposal

Such an approach is true participation in the planning process. Local decisions are being made by local people. The present writer does not believe that this is always possible, because populations of areas affected by planning proposals are some-times ephemeral, frequently do not have the money or the know-ledge to hire professional assistance, and lack either the time, education, or will to form supervisory committees to administer the implementation of plans. In the long term this kind of real participation must be our goal for all local planning. In the meantime we must take advantage of it where it is possible, stimulate it in favourable locations like council housing estates, and elsewhere make do with effective consultation.

Consultation has got itself a bad name because planners have never committed themselves to accepting the answers they get. The approach has too often been 'You tell us what you want, and we will bear it in mind in deciding what you are going to get.' The solution of this problem presents few practical difficul-ties; it is mainly a question of will. Even without central or local government legislation being passed (though that would be de-sirable) a planning department could decide that all its local plans should be prefaced by a statement of the results of its con-sultation with local people on their objectives; and that a shor-tened copy of the report (showing how the chosen plan fulfils them better than any other) be distributed to all dwellings in the locality. The consultation should take the form of an aspirations survey of all residents in small areas, and of a large sample in others, supervised by the planning department and the residents' association jointly. This procedure would ensure that local people could check at all stages that their priorities were being taken into account—by finding out from residents' association members whether or not any sleight of hand was practised in the conduct of the survey, and by seeing for themselves if the final proposals do reflect the objectives stated in the preface.

People are able to identify their critical problems and objectives at very short notice (in the space of a 5 minutes, unannounced interview), but such an approach is clearly an inadequate basis for planning proposals that may cost many millions of pounds to implement. There should be a constant cycle of information being distributed and reactions collected. Liverpool has made a small first step in pioneering this approach. In mid-1970 the planning department produced an information and issues document which was a simpler version of the report being submitted by the planners as their contribution to the annual planning programme budgeting system for allocating funds. This was widely circulated to all organisations with an interest in planning policy in the city, and to all residents, tenants and community councils, who were asked for their comments. In February 1971 the fifty-six page report[19] was condensed into a well illustrated and produced civic newspaper, which was delivered to every household in the city. If this approach had been continued—and it has not—and carried on to a more intensive level in the city's 'action areas', it could have formed a very valuable first step towards correcting the lack of knowledge of people who are at present at the mercy of corporation officials.

Before the council takes a decision on how to treat an area of, for instance, inadequate housing standards, the planning department should notify the people living there that the area's future is under review, and of the various possible actions that they could envisage. Information sheets should be supplied to each dwelling, and speakers provided for a wide range of local organisations. The residents' association should be consulted, and if none exists, efforts made to stimulate the formation of one. Finally an aspiration survey of each household should be conducted, asking such questions as:

Do you think this house is improvable?
Would you like to stay in the area or move out?
What facilities should this area have to make it a better place to
live in?
What sort of location would you like to live in?
Would you prefer to have a private garden or close access to a
public park?

Such a survey would provide a much firmer basis for the planner's brief to the architects than the usual perfunctory drawing-board mix, or the terrifying flash of divinely inspired intuition. It would not only give the council information that it needs to take a sensible decision on the way people feel about their own future; it also would enable compromise solutions to be worked out that would take account of minority as well as majority objectives.

Two problems of conflict remain. Different groups may want contradictory things. Inner ring residents may be campaigning for improvement of their social facilities, and exclusion of traffic from living areas, while suburbanites who drive their cars to work in the town centre may be actively pursuing the demolition of inner area communities to make way for new urban motorways to ease traffic congestion during the rush hours. The simple 'populist' argument of 'give the people what they want' will not work here, because we have to decide 'which people'. The obvious answer that this is a situation which must be left to the mediation of the political process is not entirely satisfactory either, since it is the recognition of their need for advice on matters such as this that causes councils to employ professionals. Certainly very few British councils would decide either to restrict private motor access to the town centre or to build an urban motorway *against* the advice of its own planners.

There are a number of ways in which such decisions about priorities can be guided. Firstly there is the conventional cost/benefit analysis, which aims to weigh all costs against the monetary value of all benefits.[20] It has a number of drawbacks, including failure of the technique to take into account *distribution* of costs and benefits in its selection of the best decision, though who pays and who profits can be shown. Equally seriously the entire calculation rests on the monetary value placed on different items, so that a high value placed on provision of social facilities for displaced families, and sound proofing of adjacent buildings, would push the calculation one way, while a high value for the time of motorists driving to work might push it to the other.

A more promising approach is to ask: 'How many people will be affected in each of the conflicting groups, and how deeply will they be affected?' Three general principles can be of help here.

1. The people most directly affected by a decision should be those whose interests are given greatest weight. And if they are hopelessly outnumbered, any proposal should attempt to find an alternative way of satisfying *their* objectives. It is not good enough for them to be told that they must suffer for the good of the majority.

2. Life-preserving and sustaining objectives, concerned with shelter, sustenance, and safety should take preference over life-enhancing ones of movement, personal fulfilment, and profit. The reason for this is that the preservation of life is a necessary precondition for its enhancement, while the reverse is not true.

3. Positive discrimination should be practised in the allocation of public resources, and in the preparation of public policies in favour of the least affluent and least competitive groups, who would otherwise be pushed into increasingly deprived conditions of life.

A Commonsense Approach to planning

Planners who have within their grasp a set of operational objectives drawn from the people who will be 'using' their plan are in the same happy position as the football team which has possession of the ball. Once a number of difficulties, not all of them predictable, are overcome, they may hope to achieve their goal. But to do this they must not only be in command of the necessary skills; they must also know the rules of the game. For the planner this means understanding the way that human values, activities and land uses relate to each other.

In the case of the contemporary production-line worker the pursuit of values may be much more indirect than it was with palaeolithic man, who hunted or collected his food and cut wattles to provide shelter, but it is just as basic.[21] In the same way all action and activities stem from attempts to satisfy values; the structures which accommodate them, and the resulting pattern of land uses, must therefore be seen as their physical expression. It is wrong to regard either activities or land uses as ends in themselves. Unless they can be shown to constitute the best way of fulfilling particular values, they are at best a waste of time, and at worst a stultifying straitjacket. The whole complex mechanism of the modern city, with all its diverse and sophisticated activities, should be no more than a device to enable its residents to fulfil as many of their values as fully as possible. This point has been neatly summarised in diagrammatic form (Fig 2) by the American planning theorist, Don Foley.[22]

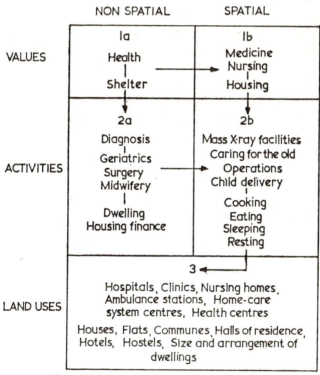

Fig 2 Values, Activities and Land Uses

The significance of Fig 2 is that land uses and structures (box 3) all stem originally from underlying abstract values or wants such as health or shelter (box 1A), which are themselves dictated by man's essential needs for food, rest, nurture and sexual activity. In the diagram they must pass through at least two stages of refinement before they take on a physical form. A general desire for health creates a demand for medical treatment (box 1B) which may be expressed in one of a number of activities including bed rest, home-care, intensive nursing or remedial physiotherapy as well as those shown in the diagram (box 2B); these in turn require certain *physical structures* (the final outcome in box 3), which will depend on the kind of *activities* that have been defined earlier as being most appropriate. An alternative route could have been taken through box 2A, linking health to its various range of component activities, and then inventing alternative physical forms to accommodate them. If we apply this construct to physical planning, we can see the processes whereby land uses are generated, and we should be discouraged from snatching at solutions in a purely intuitive way, jumping straight from value to land use without examining what alternative activities could best be employed. Another important implication is that values are only effective when they express themselves in physical activities.

These ideas could be related to planning as shown in Fig 3, which aims to show that as activities and land uses result from

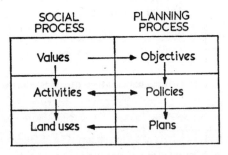

Fig 3 Social Process and Planning Process

individual and group values in the real world, so proposals and policies should flow from human and social values in the planning process. The two operations should parallel each other and be linked. People's objectives will represent the expression of their values in particular circumstances. Planning policies, designed to influence particular activities, will themselves have to take into account the nature of those activities. Finally, the developing pattern of land uses will be deeply influenced by the economic and social planning of the activities it accommodates. It is significant that two most pernicious activities—trend and inspirational planning—stem from omitting vital stages from the process. Trend planning ignores altogether the basic role of values and objectives, and simply seeks to optimise the performance of existing activities, however harmful they may be; inspirational planning fastens on an objective and devises an ideal physical solution for it, often, like Le Corbusier, with messianic fervour, without pausing to consider alternatives.

Correcting the System

When objectives have been set and the bulk of the information collected, the intelligent analysis of activities makes the introduction of a systems approach helpful.[23] The links between many major activities can be listed, and where possible given a numerical form—for example, the number of jobs needed per 1,000 adult population, or the size of rush-hour traffic flows relative to the number of people in each socio-economic group. By this means some understanding of the present situation is achieved. Assumptions can then be made about how these links (or *coefficients*) between activities will change in the future, and further assumptions can be made about one or two key factors, such as the future size and location of labour demand, or housing areas. From this an entire picture of *one* possible 'future' can be created in statistical terms. When this is contrasted with the social objectives of the strategy, crucial problems will emerge with considerable force, and potentials for desirable change can also be identified. The projections in no way indicate the directions in which we *should* be going, only what *would* be likely to happen if we allowed society to drift, or followed particular lines of action. They form a useful basis against which to work out policies for the situation we actually *want* to achieve.

Such policies must resolve conflicts not only between trends and goals but also between different objectives. This offers abundant scope for the individual's intuitive ability to solve problems. A classical example is the attempt to meet the superficially incompatible desires that most people have for company and privacy, by the design of closely packed patio houses with small enclosed back gardens, but front doors opening directly on to courtyards and pathways.[24] Where there is clear conflict between different groups or localities, a more mechanistic approach can be used, measuring the product of the numbers wanting each of the conflicting objectives, and the order of priority they accord to it. Where such an approach will not work, tests of the authenticity of objectives, described earlier in this chapter under the heading 'Consultation—A Modest Proposal' (p 63), can be applied.

We can see from Fig 3 that policies will aim to regulate activities in accordance with objectives. In order to make them sufficiently precise to indicate particular land uses, they must be refined into actual proposals. Precise standards, gathered from the analysis of information collected earlier, will make this possible. For instance, a policy concerned with the provision of a certain level of housing would have to become more detailed, eg 'The construction of 2,000 public housing dwellings and of 1,500 private dwellings a year for the next eight years, and the improvement of 5,000 public and 7,000 private ones in inner areas by the end of that period'. When such policies come to be applied to the ground, there is usually scope for alternative patterns, and these should be worked out in detail, so that they can be carefully tested against each other to see which best fulfils the plan's original objectives. As a result of this evaluation it is normally possible to marry together the best features of several of the alternatives, and thus to create a planning strategy which from beginning to end has been based on the declared objectives of the people who will be using its facilities. Implementation will take the form of a number of public interventions in the social and urban processes; development will be restricted in some areas, and encouraged in others. Local authority initiatives will lead the way in some activities such as the provision of playing fields and new industrial sites, and in others will follow on the initiatives of local people, as in the case of the improvement of the environment of the inner areas and council estates. Changing objectives, and the availability of resources, will be regularly reviewed, and the strategy amended. A precisely similar and largely parallel process will be followed in the development of local plans to implement parts of the larger strategies' objectives.

What really counts is achieving one's objectives—and not the purely secondary techniques by which one attempts to analyse problems. Objectives are neither technical nor complex; they are as familiar, and at least as crucial, to the most ill educated unemployed or manual worker as to the university professor and the managing director.

5 *How Not to Do It*

The logical failings of inspirational planning—leaping directly from general objective to total physical solution—and of trend planning—concerning itself only with the way things *are* going and not how they *should* be going—have been hinted at in the preceding chapter. It must now be emphasised that these are much more than amusing examples of muddleheadedness. They have had, and are having, the most far-reaching and harmful effects on the quality of our physical environment and social life. They are supported by planning powers of compulsory acquisition (in the UK) and eminent domain (in the USA) which would never be granted in time of peace for any activity other than planning, under its legitimising cloak of the 'public interest'. The future of our cities is being planned, with the benefit of little more public consultation than an occasional disregarded public meeting.

The Tower Block—Product of the Master Builders
Because of the well known time-lag between the development of a new technique or fashion in the USA or France and its introduction to the UK, the first high-rise flats were not built in Britain until 1948, when the London County Council laid out the much admired Roehampton Estate in parkland to the west of the city. In the succeeding two decades these perpendicular

'pillars of people' became one of the most familiar and best hated features of our urban environment.

Yet their construction continued, up till 1967, with a mounting momentum; only now is the tide receding, leaving some very ugly and sometimes unwanted debris on the urban scene. By 1966 more than half of all council housing being built in England and Wales was in blocks of flats, the vast majority of them high-rise. By comparison only 9 per cent of new *private* dwellings were flats—a sure sign that only those who had little choice could be made to live in them.[1] In that year Manchester City Council passed a resolution that no new blocks be built in the City; 4 years later the last ones, which the technical officers in the Housing Department insisted were already 'in the pipeline' at the time of the resolution, are just being completed, building having been started 2 years after it.

One of the early advocates of tower blocks was the French architect, planning visionary and technological prophet, Le Corbusier, whose obsession with technology caused him intuitively to fuse three factors—the need for circulation space for cars away from dwellings, the feasibility of developing tall buildings using newly discovered rigid-frame techniques, and the alleged desirability of space 'flowing around' buildings—to a powerful advocacy of high-rise living. In his influential, but totally inhumane, authoritarian and fanatical book *The City of Tomorrow* Le Corbusier sketched out his view of an urban utopia, which he later christened *The Radiant City*.[2] It consisted of an expanse of countrified parkland, in which were great 'living structures' incorporating shops and play centres as well as dwelling units; communication was by a network of fast landscaped freeways. When these ideas were first developed over 40 years ago, they were seized upon as an authentic glimpse of a golden future; their very failings made them more seductive. If they were simplistic, that made them easier to grasp; if they paid more attention to the needs of the motor car than the actual patterns of human interaction in the city, that was a sign of their modernity; if they completely ignored the demands of basic activities like work, play, education, commerce and dwellings for specific kinds of space, that made them revolutionary in an age which believed in revolution; if their construction was so exorbitantly expensive in demolition of existing and creation of new structures that their implementation could only be partial, that allowed their protagonists to blame their failings on the remnants of the old cities whose destruction they were planning. Architects who knew nothing of the internal workings of the most complex human creation of all—the city—set up in practice as consultant town planners.

Le Corbusier himself designed one example of his ideas a few miles outside Marseilles, a huge slab with social and shopping facilities which he called a 'Unité d' Habitation'. Occupied by families with cars, and possessing all the glamour of the great man's cachet, the Unité has worked quite well in a situation where it is the exception and not the rule. However, in a derivative way, English and American architects lacking Corbusier's technical competence, but excited as he was by the possibility of building 'living structures' instead of mundane two-storey houses, used his example as their inspiration in persuading housing and planning committees that the construction of tower blocks of flats was an act of imaginative and militant modernity. Various other makeweight arguments, which we shall look at later in this chapter, were also introduced, but it was the emotional excitement of the Radiant City movement which maintained its 40 year momentum.

Although one or two integrated structures such as the Quarry Hill flats in Leeds, and the Park Hill and Hyde Park deck structures in Sheffield, have been built (and work very well in an intensive city-centre way totally alien to the Radiant City concept), the overwhelming form that high-rise housing has taken is that of single streets stood on end, the lift shaft the smelly road, the only footpath its small waiting space. Because they are so expensive (building costs per unit are, on average, half as much again in twelve-storey blocks as on the ground), the essential social facilities of the street—play spaces, public toilets, shops and old people's sitting spaces—are not provided.[3] Although people are crowded into close physical contact with each other, there are no small informal areas to foster the casual social contacts out of which valuable friendships can develop. The young and busy only pass through public areas when they are on their ways out or in, and the old and lonely are forced to huddle in their own flats or haunt the lift area in the hope of fastening on someone to talk to.

In a nationwide social survey conducted in the UK in 1970 on the problems associated with family life in flats, W. F. Stewart found that 85 per cent of the people he interviewed would have preferred to live in a house, that 68 per cent expressed a sense of difficulty in conducting normal family life in their flats, that more than half were lonely, and that only 13 per cent expressed unqualified satisfaction with flat life. Over a half were actively dissatisfied. Of the few who were satisfied, two-thirds were in the affluent A and B social groupings. More than half of all children had to play in the house, and interviewers reported that they seemed in the main to show signs of stress and deprivation.[4] One in twelve mothers had developed nervous symptoms requiring treatment, which they attributed to flat living. Stewart particularly mentioned 'problems of isolation and loneliness and of mutual aid and co-operative action amongst the residents'.[5]

In a study of high-rise flat dwellers recently rehoused from very bad inner city slums in Glasgow, Pearl Jephcott discovered a higher level of satisfaction with the interior of the new accommodation, though there was much discontent with the exterior of the estates and their lack of services and facilities.[6] She reported universal condemnation of the flats as homes for young families, which constituted more than a quarter of the occupants.[7] The worst problems were the lack of special play, open space, and social facilities to compensate for the inherent loneliness of this type of accommodation. Though these could be partially solved by large expenditures of time and money, she concluded that high-rise living would always pose particular problems of isolation for the young and the very old, who constituted a large and increasing proportion of all council tenants.[8]

In the daytime such flats are anonymous and unsympathetic;

at night they can become dangerous. The policing of the city street by its own residents goes on day and night; lace curtains twitch, unfamiliar strangers are subjected to deep scrutiny, neighbours take a protective as well as a sanctimonious interest in each other's doings. None of this is possible in the tower block, where there are neither street nor communal facilities, and where the flats all look outwards; and the close physical proximity in which people have to live discourages them from risking any infringement of their precarious privacy. This lack of local over-sight combines with the absence of proper facilities to turn the lifts and stairs into communal urinals; vandalism is rife; and any young woman returning to her flat in the late evening runs the risk of annoyance and even assault.

As well as being dangerous and smelly, they also tend to be inconvenient, not least because lifts are frequently out of order, and one may have to wait for as much as 5 minutes in the freezing cold of the waiting space when only one lift is having to cater for all the movement in and out for sixty or seventy different dwellings. In summary, these corporation tower blocks tend to be dirty, dangerous, lonely and unloved places built at a much greater cost than the much more popular low-rise dwell-ings. They are monuments to professional arrogance, ignorance, and inhumanity, abetted by a deep lack of interest in the wishes or life-styles of their residents.

Apart from the desire to build high because the technology is there, four major reasons have been advanced to justify the tragi-farce of the tower block, all of which have been amply debunked, only to reappear as if nothing had happened. They are in descen-ding order of popularity, (1) fears of land shortage; (2) a desire to create high ratable land values, and to retain population within existing administrative boundaries; (3) the bringing back of 'life' into town centres; and (4) the importance of creating visual emphasis in new developments. In the USA the land-shortage argument is so obviously spurious that it is seldom used, but in small, relatively crowded countries like the UK, Denmark, and the Netherlands it has some apparent validity. The view from the

car seems to tell us that cities are sprawling out into the surrounding countryside, and motorways are cutting black swathes
into what is left of it. In fact, this view is partial and misleading.

The myth of the land famine

The present population of England and Wales is approxi-
mately 50 million persons, most of whom live in towns and cities
which occupy less than one-eighth of the total land surface (4.4
million acres out of a total area of 37 million acres).[9] Taking the
highest of the range population projections, it is possible that we
should want to find land for a population increase of a further
16 million persons between 1972 and the end of the century,
and that we should want to reduce existing densities and introduce new activities. Dr Stone has shown that, even assuming that
all these things result in maximum land take, this would only
consume another $1\frac{1}{2}$ million acres, or less than 5 per cent of the
remaining non-urban land.[10] Dr Best, taking an even more
extreme case, and allowing for a 10 per cent increase in the
urbanised land for each person, shows that the amount of land
needed would still be only 2 million acres or 6 per cent of the
remaining undeveloped land.[11] We simply do not have a land
shortage, either now, or in the foreseeable future.

Nor is there a major problem of diminishing agricultural output; this is rising year by year even though the area of farmed
land is very slowly contracting.[12] What is needed is better planning of the meeting points between town and country, and more
care for the environmental and aesthetic quality of the countryside, so that the illusion of a deathly cancer of urban growth
eating outwards into threatened rural environment is replaced
by a less sensational but more accurate one of healthy cities
undergoing steady and organic growth in the midst of countryside. The myth of the land famine has achieved classical proportions; as soon as one of its hydra heads is lopped off, it pops out
again elsewhere; it *is* true for its supporters (who are mainly
professionals with aesthetic tendencies) because they wish it to be
true. They fear, wrongly, that if all those at present penned into

tower blocks were allowed to live on, or near, the ground at medium densities, each with a small garden, there would be little left of the rural environment. It is thus possible for them to think themselves into the position of being the selfless guardians of the interests of future generations.

The economic argument

Councillors have often been persuaded to accept the building of tower blocks in redevelopment areas near the city centre on the grounds that such valuable land should be built at high densities to yield maximum rates to the municipality. Because of the extraordinary policy of the British Ministry of Housing (now the Department of the Environment), which has for many years disbursed much higher subsidies for local authorities building tower blocks than for those building cheaper, and more socially acceptable, low-rise dwellings, such a policy could cost the local authority no more, and in some cases even less, though the national exchequer and taxpayer had to pay the difference.[13]

The Ministry architects and administrators have, indeed, behaved with obtuseness and rigidity over the last 15 years. Not only did their financial policy encourage local authorities to concentrate on high-rise construction, but they also showed insufficient interest in the quality and suitability of the structures being erected. When the Ronan Point disaster in London occurred, killing five people and demolishing an entire block in a process of successive collapse, Ministry architects were in the embarrassing position of having to explain how this had happened to one of their recommended designs.

It is the local authority which is invariably left with the costs of maintaining and renting a very unpopular building. Salford has already approached its university to see if students can be persuaded to live in its postwar tower blocks; Liverpool, too, is also having difficulty in finding tower-block tenants. People refer to them as slums, and regard and treat them as such. It is possible that within the next 20 years there will be too few tenants left to pay for their upkeep or rates. Underlying the question of rateable value is the fallacy that concentrated development increases city income. Dwellings built elsewhere in the city, at lower densities, would yield similar rates. Perhaps existing commercial interests would like a captive market for their established city-centre shops, but they, too, can follow their customers out into new centres. And if the city has to build beyond its present boundaries, it can be confident that boundary readjustments will bring the rateable value back within a very short number of years.[14].

A further important economic argument against very high density new housing is its lack of flexibility. As Dr Stone has observed:

> It is already difficult to provide all the facilities and amenities required. and if the densities are raised further standards will fall, and it will become much more difficult to adapt the environment to future needs . . . The costs of saving land in this way are extremely high in relation to the value of the land which is saved.[15]

The search for a lost past

The oft-repeated wish 'to bring life back into the town centre' has aspects that are illogical and authoritarian. The town-centre life of a great city is not necessarily residential; indeed its most essential characteristics, such as entertainment, club life, intensity, noise, drama, anonymity, and the possibility of the unexpected, may be incompatible with the settled residence of normal families. It is neither sensible nor fair to pack people round central areas for what are in the last resort dubious aesthetic reasons. It is altogether different to make land available for private developers to erect blocks of luxury flats which can be occupied by those members of the elite who value the convenience and intensity of the location, and can compensate for the lack of space around their homes by buying it elsewhere, on rural holidays, and through frequent outings. To build high-rise council dwellings round a commercial centre is to ensure only one form of intense activity—vandalism—and one type of human contact—the abrasion of people forced to live in close proximity to each other without the lubricating effects of numerous neutral and informal meeting spaces.

None of this constitutes a general argument against all high-density housing in new or established communities. Such housing can be designed and organised to suit the lives of its residents. If recent public housing had been based on such an objective, we should probably have had dense networks of two- and three-storey dwellings grouped round courtyards, and enclosing spaces for the everyday activities which are part of the life of an attractive housing area—small shops, play areas, pocket parks, libraries and communal laundry and drying facilities. The average cost of each dwelling would have been far less than in tower blocks, and very high densities—up to two-thirds of those in tower-block development—could have been achieved. It is ironic that this is precisely the kind of housing that is being constructed in some of the more recent new towns such as Cumbernauld and Skelmersdale; people are being offered the choice of living in inhumane conditions where they are, and in many cases would like to stay, or moving to a new town to find decent housing.

Building high for effect

Unlikely as it may seem, the last of the major justifications for tower blocks is based on their appearance. Many architects still feel that a new development without a tall building is like fish without chips. To the average citizen they may seem gaunt and threatening, but in the aesthetic appraisal of the architect's scheme they may have been justified as 'forming a central point of visual emphasis' or 'providing a necessary punctuation to the development's linear rhythm'. But buildings out of the human scale are neither convenient nor reassuring. They look good only on the drawing board. Appropriate as the scale of a cooling tower is to its function of producing electric power for whole cities, we should not dream of putting one in the middle of a new residential area. As the scale of society and technology grows daily greater, it is increasingly important that we preserve in our living areas a degree of humanity, simplicity and informality, rather than creating areas which can inspire at best only awe, and at worst a sense of inferiority. By building structures as big and impressive as we can, we run the risk of creating a deathly technological environment in which successive generations become conditioned to revere size, substance and quantity, and to become alienated from their essential human nature and from the quality of natural materials.

The tower block stands condemned on economic, social, environmental and aesthetic grounds; its mushroom growth can be traced back to the cherished professional myths of architects and planners; there have also been reasons of administrative convenience, and financial attractiveness. Faced with large sites swept clean of buildings, harassed housing departments frequently took refuge in using off-the-peg layouts composed of thousands of 'units' stacked high into a number of easily located towers. Design was unnecessary, and Ministry and council alike were pleased that the slum-clearance programme was moving ahead rapidly and smoothly. One of the reasons that the resulting living environment was so unsatisfactory was that no thought had gone into its design. Because it is inappropriateness to the needs of the occupants that makes a building a slum, what was happening was that the council was pulling down cheap private slums and putting up expensive public slum environments.

A more sinister factor was the extreme profitability of the construction process for large firms, who could be sure of a continuing market for mass-produced prefabricated components paid for at a price heavily subsidised by the public purse. In the 1960s there were a number of cases where members of housing and planning committees were sent to prison for accepting cash gifts, and holiday tour bribes, for directing such contracts to particular firms. One regional representative of a large construction firm told me that they set aside 5 per cent of their project costs for such purposes.

The lessons to be learnt are that once objectives are ignored, or decided without consultation with those who will be using the final product, every kind of folly and false argument can be called in to justify irrelevant and often positively harmful technical novelties. The tower block is an abiding monument to the equation that planning minus consultation equals dictatorship of the bureautariat.

Urban Heart Transplants and Urban Death

At the time of writing very few heart-transplant patients have survived for long after the operation; rejection reactions by the old tissue caused the new heart to fail, or the patient fell prey to disorders brought on by attempts to prevent this rejection. There is a close analogy with attempts to cut out the living hearts of modern cities and replace them with new concrete transplants.

We are all familiar with the physical results of this process. One day on our way to work we notice that a shop or an office building has been vacated; soon it is boarded up, and others around follow the same course; piecemeal demolition starts. Cleared sites are surfaced with tarmac and used as short-term car parks; hoardings start to appear declaring that a large property company is developing the site as St John's or St James' Shopping Precinct; roads are closed off, enormous pieces of earthmoving equipment appear, and then the first layers of a vast concrete structure begin to rise above the rubble.

Progress is slow, and it may not be for a couple of years that the first stage of the development is opened by a visiting celebrity (appropriately enough, often a comedian) to a fanfare of praise and publicity in the local press. The first that local people know of what is in store for them is when they start to wander along the echoing channels of the new precinct, and contrast it with the complex and interesting pattern of old town-centre streets, with their wide range of specialist shops and department stores. The specialists that gave character and convenience to the town centre—the delicatessen proprietors, leather workers, cobblers, upholsterers, bespoke tailors, umbrella repairers, and the like— have been driven out, unable to pay the high rentals demanded by the investment company who have been made a gift of the town centre by the local council. The new development prospers because a new road system has been simultaneously devised to provide adjacent car parking and bus stations, and because pedestrian routes have been channelled by means of railings, ramps and underpasses, so that it is impossible to move on foot from one part of the centre to another without going through the new precinct.

Elsewhere in the town, shops and entertainment places enter a slow decline, because there is not enough custom to go round them all, and they are now relatively less accessible than the new development. The attraction of the town centre has also been diminished because of the disappearance of many of the small activities and points of interest that formerly made a visit a form of recreation, and a family outing.

A call then goes up, often from the same financial interests that have been involved in the 'redevelopment' of the town centre, for new 'out of town' shopping centres (recently christened 'hypermarkets') to cater for the increasing numbers of people who no longer wish to shop in town centres. There are many reasons for this trend, including the growing scale of the city, and the increased level of car ownership; but the planned destruction of the uniquely human, historical and diverse character of town centres also plays its part. The same drama is being enacted in many cities throughout the Western World; the citizen is a powerless spectator watching an irreplaceable urban heritage being demolished to make way for graceless concrete structures, designed only in the interests of financial gain for absentee property developers.

The machinery of the comprehensive development area
The underlying administrative process starts in one of two ways: either the council is approached by a property company with a proposal that they enter into partnership to redevelop the centre, or the local planning department decides that the central area is worn out and should be renewed. The department may then request the council to invite tenders for its redevelopment. In

practice these two approaches often converge. Alert property companies keep their eyes open for those cities whose published development plans envisage central-area redevelopment, and then approach their council with proposals to pay an agreed ground rent in return for use of the corporation's powers of compulsory purchase (or eminent domain) to acquire, demolish and lease all the land and buildings involved. (There are variants on this approach, whereby corporation and developer share both profits and costs, or where it is agreed that certain social facilities be incorporated, and their costs defrayed by lower ground rent.) A 'Comprehensive Development Area' is then designated and submitted to the Minister for his approval. He holds a public inquiry, at which those traders who do not like the idea will be allowed to put their case; but nine times out of ten the CDA is approved. Nothing can then stop the demolition of the area and replacement by yet one more covered precinct. Under the 1968 Town and Country Planning Act, the present fragile safety-catch of the Minister's public inquiry may be replaced by one conducted by the very council which has prepared the proposals.[16]

The gradual approach

There is of course nothing inherently wrong with new development in old town centres; indeed decay and renewal is an immutable law of all life as we know it. But it should be borne in mind that the heart of the city is used by a larger number of people than any other district of a similar size, and that repercussions will be felt by everyone, in all parts of the urban system. It should, therefore, be the subject of the most sensitive and delicate planning; in practice this is often largely given over to the surveyors and draughtsmen of the development company, who have only a commercial interest in the quality of the urban environment. In their drive for modernity local planners some-times even encourage developers to take over larger areas than they want, at the expense of destroying sound buildings, and under the misleading slogan of 'Comprehensiveness' the entire area is levelled.

What we are getting is piecemeal planning—for new shops and nothing else—and comprehensive demolition. What is needed is the reverse—comprehensive planning taking into account the central areas' social, cultural, aesthetic, educational, administrative and economic roles; and then, carefully regulated piecemeal redevelopment. Developers themselves might prefer the lower risks which this would involve. Small pedestrian arcades could be fitted into the town centre, where spaces could be created (as has been done in Bolton, Canterbury and Chester); and more shopping streets could be closed to traffic, as is happening in Leeds and Norwich with great success.[17] Public transport in the form of minibuses can run from car parks and bus stations through the streets closed to private cars without seriously impairing their safety—as has been proved in Leeds and Stockholm. There is no shortage of devices by which constant re-creation of the town centre can take place without the appalling destruction caused by the all-in precinct.

What is necessary as a starting point to a truly comprehensive approach to modernising town centres is a list of the uses people actually make of them, and of the things they most value in them. The town centre has for the past 25 years been treated in the USA and the UK as if it was a piece of real estate. It is so much more than that: it is the centre of life of man's most complex creation—his city.

Shops where they are needed
There is another aspect to this massive concentration of investment in central-area shopping. Few people place shopping at the top of their lists of priorities—housing, jobs, recreation and public transport usually come higher[18]—yet councils throughout Britain and the USA are spending large sums of money on acquiring expensive central sites for shopping precincts at the same time as they are cutting back on vital social services, a modern version of private affluence and public squalor.[19] Money, it is hoped, can be made out of shopping, whereas public housing, recreation and education only benefit society as a whole.

Capital investment in shopping should also in any case be re-

directed towards the growing suburbs and council estates round
the edge of the city. There is a genuine shortage of district
shopping centres which private developers are keen to meet.
Three factors are delaying their construction, all connected with
the heavy investment made by councils in central area shopping
schemes: firstly, councils are not providing incentives to encourage the opening of shops in new estates in advance of the
full build-up of population—which may take as much as 3-4
years. Those familiar with such estates know only too well the
drab sight of the young mother dragging her protesting children
across acres of mud to reach the mobile shop which constitutes
her sole source of grocery provisions. But estates departments
heavily committed to central-area schemes, and watching
anxiously to see if their investment will be justified, are under-
standably reluctant to subsidise new shops on the periphery,
which may compete with expensive new developments in the
centre.

Secondly, some planning departments are actually holding
back on the release of land for suburban shopping centres in order
to allow large central schemes to become established before
having to face increased competition. In Cardiff a citizens'
action group is fighting the corporation's plans for a huge new
shopping centre on the grounds that it is based on a grave over-
estimation of the total future shopping potential in the city, and
that, anyway, the suburban centres should be built first, because
they are more needed.[20] Thirdly, heavy commitment to new
central-area shops diverts energy, manpower and money away
from the design and construction of shopping centres near the
expanding edges of the city. Where such developments have been
built, they have been instantaneous successess, providing a local
focus in the growing metropolis. They should also be integrated
with district offices of the corporation's health, social welfare,
housing and education departments, as well as with local libraries
and bus stations. In this way a convenient administrative sub-
structure could be produced to match the city's continuing
growth, and within a short bus ride people could reach nearly

all the weekly needs of life. This would not usurp the role of the town centre, which is to supply high-order goods and services such as luxury gifts, expensive furniture, travel agencies and fashion wear.

The current plug-in precinct which is being painfully fitted to centres of western cities constitutes a classic example of how not to do it. Firstly, objectives have not been stated, discussed, analysed, or probably even considered. There has been no consultation with any of the users. Alternative uses of scarce capital have not been evaluated, nor have alternative locations for new shopping facilities. Implications for the rest of the town centre have been ignored. Finally, control of the whole development process has been handed over to concerns whose declared aim is the making of money for themselves and their shareholders, very few of whom live anywhere near the city. It is not surprising that the results are uniformly bad. Design is often brutal and clumsy, and circulation is restricted and rigid. The complexity and diversity which have grown up over centuries at the centres of towns are being destroyed at a stroke, and replaced by a drab uniformity of repetitious selling spaces. New suburbs and council estates desperately in need of new shops are being denied them; local traders are being driven out of business or faced with unfair competition; and the whole exercise is costing the cities the energy and money that should be used to tackle their real housing, transport and welfare problems.

Means Destroying Ends—The Case of the Urban Motorway
If tower blocks of flats and new concrete town centres represent prime examples of the dangers of inspirational planning, the current fashion for the urban motorway is a classical product of the wholehearted pursuit of trends. The argument is as follows. Car-ownership is increasing, the proportion of people using public transport for the daily journey to work is decreasing, and the result is steadily worsening traffic jams. If one believes that social objectives are irrelevant to planning (as technological determinists do), the logical answer is to build more roads, using

such advanced technology that they will never become prone to congestion. It is from this line of reasoning that the idea of the urban motorway developed. These are already common in the USA and Japan, and are becoming increasingly so in the UK. Of the five British cities with a population of 1 million or more, only Liverpool has not yet built its first urban motorway; work was due to start on it in 1973.

These motorways pose a number of basic problems. Because congestion primarily results from bottlenecks caused by turning traffic and intersections, motorways are designed to leap over or under all other roads, and are joined to them by complex systems of cloverleaf link roads, often termed concrete spaghetti. This makes them both heavy consumers of land, and very expensive to construct. When they are built through dense inner areas, even their high construction costs pale into relative insignificance beside those for land acquisition. Costly soundproofing is also necessary on nearby buildings, if they are not to become unusable.

The further question arises of where the vehicles are to go when they leave the motorways. By drawing them together into concentrated channels, capable of accommodating well over 50,000 vehicles in each direction in a 14 hour day, but possessing a limited number of outlet points, there is real danger of flooding the most attractive parts of the town centre with an intolerable tide of smelly and dangerous vehicles, or sacrificing large areas to multi-storey car parks. Nor is this a matter of achieving a once-and-for-all reorganisation; the construction of new roads creates further traffic; the attempt to keep up with the demands of the private motor car is doomed to failure. This is not an empty assertion. At present the majority of people working in cities still travel to work by public transport—the figure is something over 90 per cent in London, and about 85 per cent in New York, although in both cases more than half the population possess their own motor cars.[21] If urban road space is increased, more commuters will find it convenient to use their own vehicles for the journey to work, so that congestion will not be relieved, though both the environment and ease of pedestrian movement in the city will have been irreparably damaged.

Apart from these practical and economic difficulties, a question of equity is involved. The urban motorways are primarily used by commuters on their way between their suburban homes and their workplaces in the city centre; but motorway construction involves large-scale demolition of houses in the inner areas, belonging to people with much lower levels of car ownership to whom the motorways will be of little, if any, use. Even in the nearby dwellings that are not demolished, the motorways will harm the quality of life. Communities are cut up, and cross-town movements interfered with; pollution by noise (up to a distance of 150 or 200 yd) and by fumes (more insidiously but over an even wider area) must result.

There is a strong case for examining alternative solutions to the problems of urban traffic congestion; it is inevitable that such an approach should involve not only the development of convenient, comfortable and probably subsidised public transport for the journey to work, but also restrictions on the use of the private car for this purpose. Yet this is precisely what trend planners find so distasteful. Mel Webber, one of the leading advocates of permissive planning (letting technology rip), has deplored the 'elitist constraints on the use of automobiles'. He can see 'only the erosion of personal freedom at the end of that path'.[22] He does not discuss the freedom of the inner-area resident who is called upon to sacrifice his home to increase the freedom of the suburban motorist to use his car to drive to work. The wholesale folly of the tower-block era is being repeated with urban motorways. Fortunately, since we are still in the early stages, massive efforts of social and political will can still prevent the monster running the same 25 year cycle.

The scale of expenditure involved can be grasped from the estimate of the transport department of one major British city that urban motorways will cost them £5 million a mile to build.[23] This is more for 2 miles of motorway in one city than the total *national* annual subsidy for bus transport. The Greater London

Council proposed to spend more than two-thirds of its total road-construction funds up to the end of the century on building three concentric rings of urban motorways, at a total cost of nearly £2,000 million or £70 million a year for the next 30 years,[24] though the scheme has now been shelved. Since the first British urban motorway was not built till the middle 1960s, this represented a rapid and massive shift of resources, which might be thought to result from overwhelming public pressure—but this was not so. Apart from construction firms and the motoring lobby, there has not been an insistent public demand for these expensive and dangerous novelties. Britain has not yet reached the same stage as the USA, where over $8,000 million is spent every year on the construction of new freeways (an increasing proportion of it within cities), amounting to about $125 for every household in the country every year.[25] There is every reason why we should avoid doing so.

Having identified this problem, a logical planning process would have established its causes (in this case mainly the journey to work) and traced out the implications of alternative solutions to see which best matched the values and preferences of the urban population, using some form of social survey. For nearly a decade these elementary steps were not taken either by the national Ministry of Transport or local city councils. Work along these lines has been done independently by the Institute of Community Studies in London. The innermost of the GLC's proposed motorway boxes, Ringway 1, would have been built through densely populated areas, causing the demolition of large numbers of dwellings and subjecting about a quarter of a million others (within 200 yd of the new motorways) to pollution and dislocation. In this situation Willmott and Young questioned a sample of Londoners both from the inner and outer metropolitan areas to discover their three highest priorities for public spending. The two most striking facts to emerge were the low priority given to the building of new motorways, which came bottom of both lists of ten choices; and the similarity in the rankings of the two sets of people (see Table 1).[26]

TABLE I PRIORITIES FOR PUBLIC SPENDING

	GLC area per cent	Outer metropolitan area per cent	All per cent
	Respondents ranking objectives 1, 2 or 3		
Giving more help to old people	65	68	66
Building more new homes	59	51	55
Providing more recreational opportunities for young people	30	36	33
Improving secondary education	30	28	29
Controlling air pollution	26	31	28
Improving primary education	23	26	25
Improving the bus service	25	20	23
Reducing noise	18	23	20
Improving the railways and underground	15	9	13
Building new motorways inside London	9	8	8
No of people	1,102	775	1,877

It is interesting that the very people who are supposed to benefit most from new urban motorways—the residents of the outer metropolitan areas—placed a higher priority on improving public transport—20 per cent for the bus service and 9 per cent for the railways—compared with 8 per cent for roads. In the sample these two aspects received more than four times as much support as motorways.

The urban motorway has little to recommend it. It is unwanted by a majority of the population; very expensive; unjust in that its benefits are confined to the more affluent while its costs are common to all; self-defeating, because it generates more traffic than it can handle without the construction of further motorways; and ultimately destructive of the urban environment which it is supposed to serve. Its only defence, that there is no alternative, is not true. The daily tides of commuters who flood the city at morning and evening rush hours could be accommodated by existing and developing means of mass transit at much lower costs of money, disruption, amenity, and injustice (see Chapter 8).

In the USA, now entering the third decade of the urban motorway cycle, realisation of this is beginning. San Francisco's famous motorway that stops in mid-span near the city centre is a monument both to the misguided enthusiasm of its designers and the determination of the public protest group which caused its construction to be stopped. In New York a proposed West Side motorway running northwards to out of town suburbs has also been scotched by public outcry.[27] Public transport proposals are being made in a number of cities, especially New York and San Francisco themselves. In France, Paris is trying to solve its appalling congestion problems by the construction of a number of new underground metro lines, and funds have been made available for similar initiatives in Marseilles, Lyon and Bordeaux.[28] It is not enough for Western countries to turn now to public transport; the urban motorways already planned and funded must be scrapped and the funds diverted to the improvement of existing and the creation of new public transport systems.

Planning in Bits and Pieces

Tower blocks of flats, concrete town centres and disruptive urban motorways are all bad solutions because of their designers' failure to find out what their users actually wanted. They have given comprehensive planning a bad name. Numerous other examples of bad planning result from the absence of another type of consultation—that between professionals concerned with different activities in the same areas. There is no easy answer to this problem because modern mass society must rely to some extent on specialists for its education, housing, transport and social services, but their work will only be satisfactory if it is coordinated with that of each other, as well as with public preferences. Simply appointing a planning overlord will not automatically solve the problem, since he will be too remote to understand the details of the different activities to be integrated. There is no substitute for face-to-face discussions between the different departments and developers involved.

Local confusion

Most of us have at one time or another been puzzled by the prospect of new estates without shops, new towns without recreational facilities and cleared areas standing derelict and dangerous for years without any attempt being made to use them for any purpose, or even to grass them over. Local officials tend to explain that such failings are inevitable results of the problems of phasing of expenditure of different departments. Sheer repetition has tended to reduce the public to puzzled acquiescence with this view; but it must be nonsense. It is simply bad technical planning to spend money on new projects when existing ones have not been properly finished, and for this purpose the officers of local authorities must view themselves as servants of a single corporation rather than of a particular department. If the housing department has started something that requires finishing by the estates, parks and engineers departments, there should have been prior consultation with them, and commitment on the part of each to make their necessary contribution, on time. In many cases this is not happening. In human terms this means new housing estates without proper clinics, shops or parks; unscreened refuse tips, untidy derelict areas; and continued lack of basic amenities like libraries and play spaces in inner areas now scheduled for rehabilitation.

The unnecessary devastation of residential districts adjacent to clearance areas is another result of cumbrousness and inflexibility. Sites adjacent to inner areas desperately deficient in open space frequently remain rubble-strewn and undeveloped for as long as 5 years while the parks, education or housing department (for whose purposes the land is eventually earmarked) wait for their independent allocation of funds. The problem is not self-correcting, because as the redevelopment programme gets more out of phase, the delays increase. Proper coordination would have prevented the problem from arising in the first place; lack of it prevents even remedial action. Prefabricated and movable hutments and inflatable sports halls could be erected on sites which are not scheduled for use for 2-3 years, to help rectify the lack of social facilities in the surrounding communities. Apart from the money involved, the main need is for careful thought and painstaking cooperation. This would be more than justified by the resulting transformation of the quality and image of the city for residents and visitors alike.

Some developments have been carried out in an integrated way. One example is Birmingham's new satellite town of Chelmsley Wood, which was planned and designed by a unified project team drawn from a number of different departments.[29] The leader of the team happened to come from the housing department, but elsewhere he could equally be a town planner, a transport engineer, or an estates manager. Working in this kind of team ensures full use of all the information available, and improves the knowledge of each member of the kind of contribution that can be realistically expected from the various contributory departments; it also tends to create the commitment necessary to implement the final plans. This technique could also work for other projects, such as inner-area rehabilitation or the removal of traffic from local shopping centres. An added advantage is that in the long term established patterns of inter departmental hostility could be broken down, and replaced by good habits of consultation and liaison.[30]

The common element in these examples of bad planning is of the planner (whether of land use or individual activities) as know-all. The inspirational planner erects his tower blocks as quickly as he can, fearful lest consultation with a reactionary public should prevent the fulfilment of his vision. The trend planner, the devoted servant of progress, is convinced that personal preferences are simply irrelevant, or, at worst, a means of delaying the arrival of his technical millennium. The departmental warrior, bloody veteran of a dozen bitter fights with his own side, has long given up listening to anyone who does not share his own interests and jargon. And the result is an affluent and democratic society with humane principles spending vast sums of money achieving an ill finished environment, by turns trashy and drab, in which technical progress is not being matched by increasing social and personal fulfilment. Specific ways in which consultation about aims, more rigorous analysis of alternative means, and partnership in control, can help us to avoid such mistakes in future are discussed with respect to housing, communications and civic design in the following chapters.

6 Homes

Man's Struggle for Shelter

Confronted by the task of summarising in one book the experience of 10 years as a senior United Nations expert on housing, Charles Abrams selected as his title *Man's Struggle for Shelter in an Urbanizing World*.[1] It is one of the great paradoxes of the twentieth century that homelessness, overcrowding, and unhealthy housing are reaching new peaks at the same time as mankind is achieving unparalleled technological mastery over the development of resources. As the proportion of people living and working in towns continues to increase rapidly throughout the world, the competition for shelter becomes sharper, and the ideal of achieving legally acknowledged home ownership recedes further. Britain is one of the few places where even half (51.6 per cent in England and Wales) the population own their homes, so that the proud boast 'An Englishman's home is his castle' has finally become at least half true.[2]

Today's housing problems are worldwide, and the more advanced nations are not immune from them. The list is long and familiar: the notorious inner-area ghettos and squalid public housing of great American cities; the USSR's huge monotonous and yet drastically overcrowded housing schemes; the half million people living in shacks on the fringes of Paris, and the further million crowded into the slums of the inner city; and the absolute lack of shelter in the newly industrialising nations like Peru, Turkey, Nigeria, and India, where as many as a third of the people of big cities have to live in shanty towns or sleep in the open.[3-6] If, in Britain, the problems are statistically less acute, they are nonetheless very real: nearly 2 million families were living in slums at the time of a 1967 survey, and a further 2 million dwellings required improvements to bring them up to a satisfactory standard; on top of this there is a housing shortage which caused prices to leap by a half in 1971-2.[7]

These problems stem from the recent and continuing rapid growth of cities, which is in itself the product of the industrial revolutions of the last 200 years. Rural economies have been transformed into urban ones, and modern urban man can no longer follow the example of the New England philosopher Henry Thoreau who borrowed an axe and built his own house in the Spring and Summer of 1845.

Today, not even Thoreau could repeat this performance. Planning permission would probably be refused, building regulations be too stringent, and the land, anyway, be prohibitively expensive. Nor in our specialised society can the young man establishing his family call in his friends for two or three days of communal house building, to be followed by a feast, as is still done in many parts of rural Africa and Asia. Unlike the members of any other species, man no longer provides his own shelter; in densely built cities there is no place for personal idiosyncrasies, natural material (which may be prone to fire), and open-air waste disposal.

In a society of specialists such as ours the average man has neither the time nor the knowledge to build his own house. If we wish to enjoy to the full the many material and cultural benefits of such a society, we must acknowledge the heavy costs that it imposes on those who must buy from others the necessities which in a less specialised society they would produce for themselves. This is true most of all for shelter, an inescapable need and the most expensive item most people have to buy in the course of their lives.

The conclusion is clear: if we are to maintain our present form of social organisation, we must make more money available for housing, either through drastically increasing minimum-wage levels, or through more systematic and generous methods of subsidising housing for those on low incomes. While the present writer feels that the case for redistribution of income is unanswerable, all the signs are that in Britain at least there is no movement towards it.[8] While maintaining pressure on that front, we must attempt to mitigate by immediate action the worst effects both of poverty on bad housing conditions, and of expensive housing on the creation of poverty.

This is not a question of 'supporting the thriftless' but simply of acknowledging the true costs of urban living. The realisation that housing is as much a national concern as health or defence is already dawning in Britain and the USA; generous allocations of money are being channelled in both countries towards improvement of dwellings and environment in cities' inner areas, and the building of new and model cities on virgin sites, but both lack a coherent housing strategy. Boils and rashes are being plastered over, but the basic deficiencies which are causing the malady are not being rectified. In many cases they have not even been identified.

The key to developing an effective national or local housing policy is the acceptance that it must take into account the same wide range of issues that confront any family in its choice of a new home. Simply guaranteeing the mortgage, as is done in the USA, or puting up a new housing estate, as has been the practice in Britain, is not enough. Other basic factors must be taken into account, and they include repayment or rental costs, location, type of tenure, ways of matching housing design to need, access to schools, social provisions and shops, means of transport, and the maintenance or establishment of family and friendship ties.

Housing Costs

Since the most important root cause of the housing problem

is lack of resources, it might be thought that governments would have devoted much attention to discovering the most economical forms of building. Yet national and civic prestige, architectural fashion, and technological determinism have each played a larger part in design than the search for economy. This is as true in developing countries, with their model housing schemes for white-collar workers, and civil servants, as it is in the West, with its expensive obsessions with high-rise and system building, neither of which are as cheap or satisfactory as traditional two-storey housing. Recent studies show that the most economical material varies from country to country, but it is usually one produced locally; in Britain it is baked-earth bricks, and in developing tropical countries it may be either sun-dried bricks, hand-cut limestone, or locally manufactured cement.[9, 10]

The so-called 'systems' methods of construction (which involve the mass production in factories of prefabricated components for rapid assembly on site) fail to achieve the expected economies, since labour constitutes only about a third of the cost of new construction, and savings in labour costs are made at the expense of large capital investment in expensive production and movement plant. Industrialised methods are best suited to large cleared sites, where the full benefit of economies of scale can be reaped on long production runs. Even there, however, material and transport costs are relatively high, and a hitch occurring at any stage in the complex production, transport and erection sequence can cause the whole system to grind to a halt. As a result, industrialised building tends to be consistently more expensive than traditional methods—about 3 per cent, or £100 per dwelling in Britain during the 1950s and 1960s.[11]

This greater expense is not matched by higher standards. Through their inherent lack of flexibility, industrial systems exaggerate inevitable minor faults (which would be rectified by the ingenuity of a craftsman in traditional building) into expensive major failings. The John Laing company experienced such problems with its large deck-access scheme in St Mary's Ward for Oldham County Borough. Tenants soon discovered that the central heating was insensitive to individual control, and many complained of having to pay high fuel bills for being uncomfortably hot; even more serious, the window fittings were not properly sealed, and caused bad draughts. The construction company did not feel that they could rectify the fault without further payment from Oldham Corporation, and lengthy negotiations were necessary before a compromise was reached. Neither Oldham, the company nor the tenants are happy with the outcome. Runcorn New Town, which has used both system building and rationalised traditional methods, has also found that the latter are cheaper and more acceptable to tenants.[12]

Apart from high cost and poor quality of finish, there are safety reasons for avoiding system-built dwellings. Safety standards are often pared to the bone in the search for ingenious new solutions and greater economy. There have already been a number of cases of progressive collapse of panel-built blocks of flats, involving considerable loss of life.[13] The large size and common services of many such structures also contain their own dangers, as numerous recent explosions in Britain, Spain and France have shown.[14] The psychological effect of knowing that a faulty gas or electric fitting in another flat could set off an explosion that could demolish the whole building must be most disturbing to live with. Worldwide government persistence in industrialised building despite the mounting mass of information about its shortcomings, demonstrates the problem of the expert as knowall.

If the cheapest *means* of construction is a rationalised form of traditional bricks and mortar, the cheapest *form* is the terrace, deck, or row of town houses—anything in short that is low and continuous.[15] We shall see later in this chapter that these are the very characteristics that many of those needing homes most value. Such types of house are also economical in their use of land, allowing every family to have a small garden without locking up excessive areas in unwanted and ill-tended large gardens, or wastefully extending roads and services. There are other social and environmental advantages, too, such as coherence, compactness and convenience, enclosure, and ease of separating pedestrians and vehicles.

The green noose

The cost of building land is not the dominant element in the final selling price of a house, of which it seldom constitutes more than one-quarter, but where there is a famine of housing land, and a resultant shortage of new dwellings being built, house prices rise sharply in response to the laws of supply and demand.[16] Thus land-use planning exerts a strong influence on housing costs by controlling the supply of housing land. In both Britain and America in the last 25 years planners have been guilty of mismanaging this land market. In Britain it has taken the form of a so-called Green Belt policy—the designation of continuous and wide rings of land round great cities in which little or no development is allowed. As the natural growth of the city has continued, pressure and land values have increased dramatically inside the Green Belt, and those who could afford it have escaped into commuter settlements beyond. Finally bits and pieces of land at the inner edges have been sacrificed to urban growth, so that it has become an expanding noose, tight enough to keep the victim in a state of constant distress without actually killing him. There is much to be said in favour of preserving recreational, agricultural and amenity areas close to great cities; the mistake of the Green Belt was to attempt to frustrate totally, rather than to channel, urban growth. Green Zones, allocated for specific activities, would be far more effective in maintaining access to the countryside for the people of the city than constantly retreating Green Belts; and at the same time they would leave room for natural urban growth.

The recent development of the Manchester conurbation shows how beneficial this approach can be. Although the greatest pressures for housing land have been to the south of the city on the lush pastures of the Cheshire Plain, development has been held in check in this area and diverted towards the old industrial towns on the northern side, which were beginning

to loose their populations, and starting on a downward spiral
in land values and urban services that could ultimately have led
to their becoming ghost towns. Instead they are being rapidly developed for medium-priced private housing. New capital has
been invested in the town centres of Bolton and Bury (whose
future was regarded as unpredictable a decade ago) and into
residential development round the old coal and cotton communities of Royton, Chadderton, and Rawtenstall, which had been
beginning to decay. These tides of newcomers have been welcomed because their arrival ensures continued use and support
for existing urban facilities, whereas the towns within and beyond
the Cheshire Green Belt to the South of Manchester have experienced major problems in providing basic services like education and sewerage for their rapidly increasing and fertile young
populations. Had planning restrictions not existed, they would
have faced breakdown, and the old towns of the north decay or
even dereliction.

In this instance restriction has worked well, because there
existed by happy accident large alternative areas of housing land.
But in other places like London, Liverpool, and Birmingham,
the result has been disastrous in human terms. Two years after
the Milner Holland Report (dealing with the plight of poor
families forced to live in London to be near their work) pointed
out that the critical problem was the lack of dwellings, the
planning department of an adjacent county, Kent, was still
vigorously opposing any incursions into the proposed Green
Belts, which covered much of the county, and did all they could
to 'hold the Green Belt' against repeated requests for more
housing land for London. They were incensed when the Minister,
R. H. S. Crossman, overturned one of their decisions in 1965 and
allowed a tiny development to proceed inside the holy area—the
village of New Ash Green about 300 acres—to accommodate the
families of 2,000 commuters. The truth of the matter is that
Green Belts create famines of housing land where it is most
needed, and force up house prices so that only the affluent can

afford decent accommodation within the city, or the high cost of daily commuting.

As pressure for more housing land builds up inside the Green Belt, the number of applications to develop disjointed areas on its inner edge increases, and these are frequently allowed on appeal to the Secretary of State because each case must be considered on its merits, and appellants can often point to acute housing shortages in the vicinity. This kind of erosion happens on a larger scale with council housing developments, like Liverpool's Speke, Kirkby, Cantrill Farm, Halewood and Netherley estates, all of which were built over a period of twenty years within, or adjacent to, a proposed Green Belt. Each was planned as an urban cul de sac isolated from the others; because of uncertainty at the time as to whether further land could be obtained, housing densities were pushed up as high as possible. In some cases as many as half of the dwellings were in tower blocks, further increasing their physical isolation. Although the Green Belt was pushed further back, the practice had harmful effects and did not protect the land it was intended to safeguard. It would be better if plans were to be concentrated on safeguarding really precious agricultural, recreational and scenic areas at the same time as ensuring that there was sufficient room elsewhere for the continuous growth of the homes, shops, and workplaces of the expanding population of the metropolis.

The zoning game or get back to the ghetto

As befits its political traditions, the US version of the same approach relies more on local initiative and less on centralised policy. It is a hundred-headed hydra rather than the one-eyed cyclops monster of the British Green Belt, and it will be far more difficult to destroy. American local authorities are allowed to impose their own zoning regulations. Thus affluent suburbs round the fringes of great cities zone their spare land for residential development at densities of four or five dwellings to the acre, and refuse planning permission to schemes at higher densities

which would allow in less affluent people. Their attitude to the
non-elect is quite simply that which Dean Swift attributed to the
Calvinists :

We are the chosen few,
All others must be damned,
There is no room in heaven for you,
We can't have heaven crammed.

The crisis of the ghetto must be met, at least in part, in the
outer suburbs. One significant attempt to achieve this is being
made by Suburban Action Institute, whose directors, Paul and
Linda Davidoff and Louis Gold, aim to challenge restrictive
suburban zoning regulations in the courts on the grounds that
they are illegal under the equal opportunity provisions in the
constitution.[17] A complementary approach is being adopted by
the New York State Urban Development Corporation, which is
trying to buy large slices of suburban land for the construction
of high-density public housing.[18] Both approaches are in their
infancy, and though the actual numbers of people rehoused in
the suburbs are so far small, they have already aroused the bitter
hostility of those who see their arrival as an invasion.

Lightening the debt burden

For most householders repayment of interest is responsible for
about half their housing costs. The council-house tenant is helping to repay the loan that enabled the local authority to pay for
his dwelling in the first place. The private-house buyer has in
most cases borrowed the money, say from a building society, and
is repaying it over a period of 20-30 years at a rate between 8 and
10 per cent, so that in all he is paying for twice the original
value of the house. There is no magical political or economic
solution to this problem; the building of any structure in any
society is going to involve the use of time and materials that
could otherwise be put to another productive use. The payment
of interest means that the people who are enjoying the use of

the house, rather than society as a whole, pay for diversion of resources—what economists call the 'opportunity cost.' If government made the money available, interest-free, out of taxes, the
opportunity costs would be distributed differently, but they would
not disappear. There is a strong case for doing this in unequal
societies like our own, to ensure that no families are deprived of
adequate shelter because of their poverty, and until recently
Britain's council-housing subsidies of about £250 million per year
(or £44 per council dwelling) have aimed to do this.[19] Even
under the system introduced by the Conservative Government
in 1972, people on very low incomes living in council property
receive rent rebates, which should redistribute some of their
housing costs on to existing council tenants with incomes above
a certain level. The way it is being done is cumbersome, inefficient,
invidious, humiliating and mean, and is an example of the bad
results of the halfhearted application of the good principle of
subsidised housing.[20] The subsidy to those who are buying their
own homes, on the other hand, takes the form of exemption from
income tax on their mortgage repayments, and amounts to an
average value of about £46 per year.[21] By contrast with rent
rebates it is very easy to claim, involves disclosure of the minimum amount of personal information, is not means-tested, and
does not need an army of civil servants.

Desirable as it may be to redistribute part of the housing costs
of the poor throughout society, it is still advantageous to reduce
as far as possible the national burden of interest repayment for
house building. The only ways in which this can be done are to
build cheaper houses or to improve old ones instead of demolishing and replacing them.

Of the 6 million dwellings in England and Wales built before
1919, fewer than 2 million are slums; the remainder are decent
terrace houses designed for the expanding classes of artisans and
clerks in the building boom of the late 1890s, and spacious
Edwardian semi-detached, detached, and town houses. Although
basically sound, many need improvement and repair if they are
to play their part in solving the country's present housing pro-

blem. The sums involved are moderate; a 1967 survey carried
out by the Department of the Environment showed that nearly
a third of these dwellings needed less than £125 spending on
them, a further 40 per cent less than £500, and only a quarter
more than that.[22] In short, there are $4\frac{1}{4}$ million older dwellings
which, given the expenditure of small sums of money of up to
£500 on each, could continue to provide very adequate and
relatively cheap shelter, but which, if ignored, could rapidly
deteriorate into slums. In addition many of the council houses
built between 1919 and 1939 are now in need of improvement
and repair, and the number of such properties receiving this
treatment is in fact increasing (by a third between 1969 and
1970 to 40,000).[23] If this rate were to be doubled to 80,000 a
year (and there are signs that it will be), all the 1 million inter-
war council houses in need of modernisation will have been dealt
with by 1984, by which time the postwar stock will be ready
for attention.

The real problem focuses around the $4\frac{1}{4}$ million vulnerable
pre-1919 dwellings which are not scheduled for slum clearance.
Action on the $1\frac{3}{4}$ million requiring less than £125 of repairs can
be safely left for the time being, so that the problem becomes one
of improving the remaining $2\frac{1}{2}$ million older dwellings within
the next 10 years, which would require an average rate of 250,000
improved private dwellings every year. This was nearly achieved
for the first time in 1972, partly by the massive exploitation of
the system by large property companies.[24] If the loopholes in the
legislation are closed, and the organisation of local authorities'
housing improvement sections strengthened, there is no reason
why these high rates could not be maintained without large
numbers of sitting tenants being evicted, as at present.

The alternative to such a policy—the clearance and replacement of older dwellings and areas by new ones—is unsatisfactory
on three grounds. Firstly, it is impracticable because the current
rate of new house construction is inadequate to replace our
existing 2 million slums and provide the 1–$1\frac{1}{2}$ million new dwellings that will be needed to accommodate new households in the

next 10 years, let alone cure England and Wales' existing deficiency of 330,000 dwellings—for which 350,000 dwellings a year would have to be built. The figure is 50,000 short of that and the trend is downwards.[25] We cannot pull down all the older homes and replace them with new ones. Secondly, there are important human reasons for preferring improvement to massive clearance. Community feeling and mutual support are products of time and shared experience; over the years a neighbourhood becomes more than the sum of all the families living there; numerous studies have shown that the mixture of generations is of value to each, and that the certainty of support from friends and relations in good times and bad is often missed by the people of such areas when they are rehoused on new estates.[26]

Thirdly, there are cogent economic advantages; these have been explained in detail by Stone and Needleman, and relate to the dramatic saving on interest that can be made by the lower capital costs of improvement.[27] Basing his calculations on the 1967 situation Needleman showed that it was advantageous for society as a whole to spend the following amounts on improving houses with certain remaining lives, assuming the stated interest rates (see Table 2).

TABLE 2 JUSTIFIABLE IMPROVEMENT COSTS PER DWELLING, AS PERCENTAGE OF COSTS OF REBUILDING

Remaining life of improved dwelling in years	Prevailing Rate of Interest					
	4%	5%	6%	7%	8%	9%
15	29	37	45	51	56	61
30	45	55	63	69	74	78

Since this calculation was done, the cost of new dwellings has increased by a half, so that the figures of justifiable expenditure are now even higher. By making available improvement grants of 50 per cent and higher, central government is beginning to recognise the important role that older dwellings can play in keeping down new housing costs. General Improvement Areas are now being designated by local-authority planning departments, and central government is giving grants of up to £200 per house for environmental improvements, to make sure that the effect of money spent on the houses is not diminished by the depressing impact of a drab environment.

Unfortunately the simple provision of the cash is not proving sufficient. Local authorities are unwilling to take on the work inside their own direct works departments for fear, presumably, of being unable to cope; but nor do they have the administrative expertise to process simply and efficiently applications for grants to individuals using private surveyors and builders. A further problem arises from the fact that both architecture and surveying are lucrative professions, whose practitioners demand the same percentage for designing a standard back-bedroom/bathroom conversion as for an entirely original dwelling. Local authorities will have to employ architects and surveyors directly, and put them in charge of teams of draughtsmen and clerks to carry out the design and administrative aspects of housing improvement. A small charge can be incorporated in the improvement costs; and will be more than offset by the saving in the subsequent costs of rehabilitation over replacement.

The fact that organisation as well as money is needed is emphasised by the dramatic failure of the urban rehabilitation provisions in the 1968 US Housing Act which made 100 per cent mortgage guarantees available to poor families buying their own homes in the inner city. The hope was that they would then devote personal care to their maintenance and improvement. In fact, lack of oversight and real involvement of local authority teams in achieving change on the ground has resulted in a paper operation, allegedly riddled with fraud and estimated to have cost the Federal Government $200 million in reneged mortgages.[28] Fraud cases have been brought against real-estate lawyers and Federal housing officials in Philadelphia, Boston, St Louis, Chicago and Miami; in New York a Federal Grand Jury handed down a 500-count indictment against a large group of operators, alleging a conspiracy to defraud the government. Because there were no improvements to the houses' environments new owners had little incentive to put money into their properties. The condition of many of them was anyway so bad that they would never have been the subject of a mortgage guarantee if the real-estate operators had not bribed the officials concerned.

The British approach of declaring General Improvement Areas in which £100 or £200 a dwelling is available for environmental improvements (to be installed by the local authority) is better, as is the technique of giving grants to cover half or more of the costs of specific improvements, payable to the builder on completion. Although the organisational reforms outlined above are overdue, some success has already been achieved. Within 2 years of the procedure being introduced in Britain's 1968 Housing Act, 112 different local authorities had designated 143 General Improvement Areas containing 40,000 dwellings, for which 2,563 improvement grants had been approved in a single year.[29] To be fully effective, the scale of these operations will have to be increased by about fifty-fold, but a promising start has been made.

A housekeeping policy for homes

By drawing together these arguments on construction, land and improvement costs, we can develop a strategy to keep total housing expenditure down to the lowest level compatible with providing suitable shelter. Britain should firstly replace the Green Belts by a series of safeguarded recreational, amenity and agricultural areas; between these, land should be made available to accommodate the growth of cities. This would ensure a steady supply of cheaper land for building the 2-3 million extra homes Britain will certainly need in the next 20 years. High building and system building must be avoided, for economic as well as social reasons. Rationalised traditional methods should be employed instead, to build high-density but low-rise continuous terraces of town houses, and the courtyard developments that many families from clearance areas prefer. Simultaneously, equal numbers of older dwellings should be improved—about 300,000 a year—using local authority technical staff and direct-works departments, and small private builders. It is only by such a combined policy of construction and improvement that housing supply can be brought to exceed demand by the 5-6 per cent necessary to keep house prices stable and allow families to move freely from one place to another.

Living Cities and Garden Suburbs

The champions of the intense life of the inner city, and those of the more spacious and rural environment of the outer suburb or garden city, have been at each other's throats for many years. Accusations of sentimentality, authoritarianism and ignorance have been hurled with equal force in both directions. Theorists like Jane Jacobs[30] have eloquently stated the arguments for preserving the traditional city, and many who care deeply for the welfare of their fellow human beings, like Arthur Dooley, the Liverpool sculptor, share her feelings.

Dooley argues that if all the cleared land in the city were developed with the kind of dense low-rise courtyard dwellings also favoured by the present writer, there would be no need for new towns or peripheral estates. His argument is supported by the fact that in the 10 years between 1961 and 1971 Liverpool's population declined by over 20 per cent (130,000 people), and the wider conurbation also lost 120,000 people, which was more than equalled by the *increases* in the population of the surrounding rural districts.[31] No one can doubt that there have been appalling failures in the planning of the city during this period; basic lack of coordination and programming has meant that cleared sites have stood, and are standing, idle; structurally sound large Victorian dwellings have been, and are being, condemned because overcrowding has led to bad health conditions— but their demolition can only increase overcrowding elsewhere. Dooley and Jacobs, and all those who decry the planners' squandering of unique civic heritages, are incontestably right, but their proposals for the *future* are not always fully reliable.

Their vision of an intense interacting city built on the human scale, whose sequences of small linked spaces are dominated by people and not machines for moving, working or living in, and which relies on clean and cheap public transport and has con-

fined the motor car to a certain number of designated roads—
such a vision is authentic, and completely practicable. But there is
not room in our existing cities, even if thus organised, for all
the new households that are constantly being formed by the slow
but steady increase of population.

The industrial slums being cleared were built at average net
densities of about twenty-eight dwellings to the acre (and in their
case net and gross densities are similar because of the scarcity of
open spaces or communal facilities).[32] The net density of modern
local-authority housing is much less than that, only 18 dwellings
to the acre, and though (in the present writer's opinion) this
could be increased with greater ingenuity and care in design, it
is unlikely that densities could be raised by much more than a
quarter (to about 24 dwellings to the acre) without some families
being forced to live off the ground.[33] By the time shops, schools,
play and circulation space, and other modern urban facilities
have been included, gross densities will have fallen to about 12
dwellings to the acre, rather less than half the gross density of the
slums being cleared. This means that land will have to be found
outside existing built-up areas for replacements of about 1 million
of the 1,800,000 existing slums. Over 80,000 acres (or
125 sq miles) of new housing land will have to be found for this
purpose alone.

Natural increase of the population will create further demands,
even at present low levels of growth. All those who will be forming
separate households in the next decade are already born, and we
know for certain that in the period 1971-81 there will be at least
another 1 million households to accommodate, needing a further
125 square miles of housing land.[34] Such demands should not
frighten us because the combined total would not consume more
than half of 1 per cent of the available land; but it does mean
that we must look outside the confines of existing cities for at
least part of the answer to urban problems.

Now that the dust is beginning to settle, it is becoming clear
that the fierce battle of words between the Living City and
Garden Suburb champions was not necessary.

No sensible enthusiast for New Towns would deny the crucial

importance to Western civilisation and ways of life of maintaining vital inner cities. Equally, no embattled defender of the city, when confronted by the impossibility of squeezing all a growing population into existing urban areas, would oppose the creation of alternative environments. For the vision of the Garden City is authentic, too. It is easier in a green-field site to create a natural environment of foliage, fresh air and moving water, in which individuals can feel the rhythm of the changing seasons, than in the intensely urbanised inner areas of old cities. This is particularly important for those with young families. In their study of families moving from Bethnal Green (a cramped but lively part of London's East End) to Greenleigh (an overspill estate in open country 20 miles out from the centre), Young and Willmott[35] reported that Greenleigh's semi-rural character was particularly appreciated by those with families. It must be stressed that Young and Willmott also discovered widespread discontent with the lack of social life and facilities in the new estate, and commented cogently on the disruption of existing social ties which resulted from the move.

Until recently, the only essential feature built in such areas on time was the school—and this because it was a legal responsibility. Clinics might follow a year after the first residents moved in, a few shops in the second year, but not a complete range until the entire estate was occupied, as much as 5-6 years later again. Other essential recreational, cultural and entertainment facilities were frequently ignored. This deplorable, perfunctory and inefficient planning should not be tolerated. In countries such as the Netherlands and Sweden, shopping, social, medical and cultural facilities in New Towns are subsidised by central government, to the extent of making them national showpieces.[36] If people are moving away from close-knit localities in which they grow up to totally new places inhabited entirely by strangers, they need more, rather than fewer, communal facilities.

The over-cautious approach of not meeting most needs until the full 'economic' level of demand has built up has transformed British New Towns (which enjoyed great initial public support) from being a symbol of social progress to one of social alienation and massive discontent; but it is not too late to rectify the mistake by bringing forward expenditure that will have to be incurred anyway.

Planning for Choice

Nationally

It seems likely that all the following policies will be necessary if Britain's housing problems are to be solved:

1. much more intensive and careful redevelopment of cleared sites in inner cities;

2. a continuation of present new and expanded town policy, but concentrating in future on quality rather than speed (why rush to rehouse people in heartless and inconvenient surroundings?);

3. development of new edge-of-town estates as coherent garden suburbs focused around unified social, shopping and administrative centres, with funded provision for subsidised public transport;

4. concentration on improvement rather than clearance of the $4\frac{1}{4}$ million sound dwellings built prior to 1919.

The relative emphasis that should be given to these four complementary policies can only be decided by discovering the preferences of the people concerned—those in the clearance areas of inner cities, and the young, aged 14 to 20, who will be setting up their own homes for the first time in the next 6-10 years. There are a number of official bodies well fitted to do this role of vital social reporting; they include the Central Statistical Office, the Government Social Survey, and the Office of Population and Census Surveys.[37] Knowledge of the housing priorities of all sections of the community would be valuable, and a 1 in 1,000 sample national survey would be perfectly practicable for the OPCS, well versed in the conduct of much larger exercises. If such a survey were conducted every 5 years, changing priorities could be charted. Between such major surveys, more intensive ones of smaller areas or groups could provide information on the proportions of different age and social groups preferring particular housing locations, types and densities.

Locally

Consultation can include not only residents' and tenants' associations but also the schoolchildren who will be forming their own families within the next 5-10 years (about the length of time it takes for a housing scheme to progress from first thought to first occupants). Apart from complaints and abuse in the press, local-authority planning and housing officials have no means of knowing the preferences of their future clients for any aspect of housing—where, what, how big, how organised, what size of garden, if any, or what kind of access. No design can meet all the clients' objectives perfectly; some of them will conflict. The design process consists of finding physical forms that subordinate less important to more important objectives. If, for instance, it emerged from research and consultation that the highest priority of most people in a city's clearance area was to live in two-storey dwellings, and that the second priority was to stay within easy reach of the existing town centre, though not necessarily within their present locality, a logical design process would produce some solution that involved high-density low-rise accommodation as close to the city centre as possible, either on a cleared inner-area site or at the city's edge; and public-transport proposals would be submitted to the relevant department and committee of the corporation. At each successive stage of the scheme's development, new design questions would arise and could be answered in the same way. Indeed the district offices of corporation housing departments should see the collection of information about the good and bad design points of recently built dwellings as one of their most important jobs, both for present management and future design. Those who have lived in corporation estates will be familiar with problems arising from lack of detailed knowledge on the part of the designer—badly placed or non-existent airing cupboards, awkward kitchens, inadequate storage space.

The problem is well known and crops up at most housing conferences. Kitchens give a good illustration of it. They are designed by architects as spaces for the preparation of food, and built by contractors for whom they are the terminal points of a number of water and power ducts. The women who will spend much of their waking lives in them are not consulted. Local-authority architects rely on the annual publications of the London-based Central Housing Advisory Committee, composed entirely of experts, largely male and few of them cooks, or on articles in architects' journals, to discover the preferences of people whom they could consult directly in their own localities. The resultant design may be theoretically adequate but in fact unpleasant.[38]

In isolated instances alternative approaches have been tried with great success. In Newcastle-upon-Tyne, Vernon Gracie has designed a unit of 46 old-people's houses and flats in consultation with those who were to be their first occupants. He also lived in the area for 2 years while working on the scheme. There were regular meetings with the prospective residents and with councillors to decide on general layout, number of rooms, siting of cupboards, power points, internal colour schemes and the types of fences around gardens.[39] The average cost of the dwellings (£4,600 each, including land and landscaping) has not been above average, but the satisfaction of the residents has. Such an approach if used widely on the local scale could lend renewed intimacy and relevance to housing-improvement areas, and endow new public housing with a degree of convenience and acceptability that is too often lacking.

Burning the formulas

Most public housing in Britain is designed by formula—the 'mix' of different house types and numbers of rooms are both laid down by the director of housing for each city, and faithfully reproduced on each new estate, irrespective of the composition of the families to live there. It is difficult to apportion blame for this ludicrous state of affairs between planners who do not insist on providing a sensible brief for the housing and architects' departments to work to, and these departments themselves, which do not ask for one. But the omission of thorough social surveys has more far-reaching effects. It means that architects are designing for clients whom they have not only never met but of whom they do not even have a reliable impression. So council-house designs are either repetitious or capricious; they undergo fashions as silly as those that affect women's clothing—keyhole closes, tower blocks, short maisonette blocks, deck-access spine blocks—each holds the field for a few brief years, only to be replaced by a new fad when its shortcomings are exposed. This restless and ineffectual experimentation is not necessary. All but the small proportion of mentally retarded are capable of ordering their housing priorities in logical terms. A preliminary checklist which families could rank in order of preferences might read as follows:

> possession of a small garden/large garden
> access to shops, and to schools
> availability of play space nearby
> living on the ground
> having a good view
> privacy
> neighbourliness
> low rent
> adjacent garage for car
> safety of environment for children
> access to large open spaces.

By processing the priority given to such objectives, it is possible to obtain logical starting points for the design process. This is already standard practice amongst architects designing for private clients; there is every reason why it should also be applied to the considerably more important and challenging tasks of designing whole estates and neighbourhoods for thousands of families.

Implementing a National Housing Policy

One of the basic problems confronting any housing policy in a mixed economy is the difficulty of persuading private builders to accept it. Government can set target figures of numbers of dwellings to be built, but it cannot ensure that they will be met or that developers will consent to build where administrators think best. This problem can best be tackled by central and local government building houses for sale, in the same way as is already planned for a number of new towns, including Milton Keynes, Warrington, and Central Lancashire New City.[40] At the moment local authorities in England and Wales build few houses for sale—only 585 in 1970—but they could be encouraged to do so, using 100 per cent central government loans for finance and private building firms for construction.[41] Taking part of this entrepreneurial role away from private enterprise would prevent the violent fluctuations of building rates that have resulted in recent years from uncertainty on the part of the building industry about the future of both government policy and of the market; and it would put the guidance of building programmes into the hands of the same people (the local-authority planners) who are charged with estimating an area's future housing need. The integrated design of privately owned and publicly rented housing areas could be improved, and economies made by providing joint shopping and social facilities, which is seldom possible at present.

As the level of mobility necessary for the efficient working of a modern society continues to rise, so does the proportion of extra houses needed to allow people to find a suitable dwelling when moving. Theorists already argue that it should be as high as 5 per cent, as against the 2 per cent so far achieved in England and Wales.[42] This means that nearly a million more dwellings than households could be provided before supply would start to exceed demand.

Exchanging vital statistics

Not only must administrators know what potential occupants want; the potential occupants must have access to information on

alternative types of accommodation. At the moment, the more
acute a family's housing need, the more difficult it is for them to
get this information. Private estate agents are seldom helpful to
people looking for cheap rented housing, both because there is
little money to be made from them and because they suspect
their ability to maintain payments. Nor can such people often
raise the down payment on a mortgage (which is higher for
those with low incomes than for richer people). Council housing
departments have traditionally been cavalier with inquirers,
seeing their responsibility as ending with the addition of people's
names at the bottom of the housing list, and with notifying them
(often several years later) when and where they can be offered
a letting. The disadvantages of this situation have led to the
recent establishment of housing advice centres in New York and
London. [43, 44]

In a number of New York districts, housing, welfare and
cleansing officials all work from the same building, or 'neighbourhood city hall', which may also house local community organisations. In the London borough of Lambeth a new Department of
Housing Services has been created to help with a wide range
of issues, including landlord relations, public-health requirements,
building society and council mortgages, and the buying, selling,
renting, conversion and improvement of private properties, as
well as all aspects of municipal housing, especially transfers and
rent rebates.[45]

Many local authorities in Britain and the USA are much
larger than Lambeth, and new public housing estates may be as
much as 6 or 7 miles away from the municipal offices, so that no
single central housing office would be adequate. Special local
ones are being established in areas of particular housing stress in
Manchester, and in Liverpool's Granby Ward, where it is hoped
that social services, public-health and cleansing staff will eventually join the existing housing officials and voluntary workers.

Conclusion
In any free society one of the most important questions that a

housing policy must face is 'Does it offer individuals a real range of choices?' By concentrating on low building in traditional materials, and preventing famines of building land by abandoning Green Belts, it should be possible to stabilise house prices, so that the basic problem 'Can I *afford* to choose?' will not be so critical.

Early building of social and recreational facilities in new housing areas will do much to prevent recurrence of 'New Town blues', particularly if the residents are, in future, families who have selected a New Town as their first preference. In parallel with this creation of new communities must go a conscious resurrection of the older cities, which have formed the cradle of our current culture but which are in many cases showing serious signs of decline. Intensive redevelopment of slum sites with dense and intimate networks of modern dwellings would help re-create their traditional vitality without perpetuating bad living conditions; surrounding such areas, the dignified districts of Victorian and Edwardian artisans' dwellings must be improved through the active intervention of local authorities and with the full participation of local residents, if they, too, are to avoid becoming slums.

Achieving a correct balance and thus ensuring effective choice for the individual must depend on a triple strategy of consultation at national, municipal and local level. National surveys of housing problems and preferences can provide objectives for relevant policies, and these can be regularly updated and redirected to match changing conditions and aspirations. Local authorities can accept their responsibility for maintaining in good heart the total housing stock, and for ensuring sound and suitable accommodation for present and future residents. This will demand a great improvement in management, both in seeing that environmental and housing improvements go hand in hand, and in organising and implementing the result of consultation with existing residents' and tenants' associations, and with the young people who will be the householders of the future. Finally, at the local scale, there should be readily accessible housing aid centres, preferably in the same building as other corporation departments, to which residents, tenants and owner-occupiers alike can take their housing problems. This will do much to end the long and unprofitable history of conflict between councils and residents' associations; and between departments and the people they exist to serve.

7 *Physical Communications*

One of the major problems of modern communications is the confusion in the minds of many between the elusive qualities of life for which they are seeking and the tangible communications which they hope will transport them into this dream world. Sweeping down the urban motorway by car becomes strongly associated with the ability to rediscover the half-imaginary and secret wonderlands of childhood. As personal demands for space rise, the path into the relatively open hinterland becomes more highly prized as an escape route, almost a lifeline. But the very car which seems to offer access to the unspoilt beauties of natural surroundings, and is the main element in the rhythmic tides of evening and weekend traffic out of the city, contributes drastically to the destruction of the urban environment. Nor is there any self-regulation in the demand for more cars and roads; if the pursuit of nature brings one only to a new estate, or a national park crawling with other cars, then the demand is raised for more urban and rural motorways to cater for the increased traffic that they have themselves generated.

The most destructive form of travel today is the car used for the daily journey to work from outer suburb to city centre. The populations of the older parts of great cities throughout the Western World are declining, both because of the flight to the suburbs and because housing land is increasingly being taken for other purposes, particularly for new urban motorways.[1, 2]

The city centre, which is the end of most journeys, is being sacrificed to 'improve' the means by which the journey to it is made.

The City as Route Maker

Specialisation of function, which became the hallmark and major ingredient of the success of the city, could not have developed had there not been routes along which its particular products and the agricultural output of its hinterland could be transported. Though the city may have started as a military or religious settlement, it grew as a market, and the focus of specialists, dependent upon importing their materials and exporting their products. So the road has contributed much to the city, particularly to its rapid growth and continuing dynamism; but settlements have done even more for roads—they have created them. When the building of roads begins to clash with the welfare of the cities they are supposed to serve, the tail is beginning to wag the dog.

None of this is to deny that moving around can be an important and intrinsically enjoyable part of life. Ability to move has always been a significant factor in an individual's freedom. In the modern world increasing personal mobility is still enlarging freedom and choice; large numbers of people engaged in repetitive and uncreative work in production-line factories, and living in cramped accommodation, are able to escape at weekends in their own cars to pursue the same dream of rural purity and peace as is sought by the affluent managers and shareholders for whom they work.

The existence of good communications also widens the individual's effective range of possible jobs, his wife's choice of shops, and his children's educational opportunities. Certain American theorists think that the increasing speed of physical and electronic communications will bring about basic changes in the conduct of community life and the organisation of society: when people have the opportunity to choose from a wider range of contacts, present local-scale patterns of association will be replaced by national, and even international, ones. They also think that in the society of the immediate future stability will be replaced by dynamism, with people commuting scores of miles to work, play and relax, at very high speeds, and also moving their homes at much shorter intervals.[3] This line of thought seems to be highly speculative, and to be only relevant in the foreseeable future to the members of small elites. Nevertheless there is a noticeable contraction of world and national scales; mobility and interaction are increasing, in the small country town as much as in the great metropolis. Though many factors play their part in this change, improving communications are the crucial element. Where human contact and personal choice are being enhanced, the results are beneficial, but where these values are being frustrated, and the quality of urban life is threatened, then we are indulging in mere speed for its own sake. And whatever the technological enthusiasts and futurologists may say, there is no sense in that.

The Problem of Urban Traffic—Big Streams, Little Channels
The crux of the transport problems of modern industrial societies lies within cities. Their commercial, industrial and residential areas generate and attract traffic. Flows *between* cities cause relatively few problems: in many cases good railway services exist, and can be made to run at a profit;[4] new motorways can be built from the outskirts of one city to those of the next with relatively slight dislocation of existing rural activities; and helicopters, aeroplanes and pipelines transport increasing volumes of traffic and freight from one part of a country to another.

City traffic poses more intractable problems: firstly, those of fitting regional and even national flows into narrow and rigid urban channels; secondly, those of accommodating the enormous daily tides of people journeying to and from their workplaces; and thirdly, those of maintaining the links between activities in different parts of the growing metropolis. Since 1945 there has been a phenomenal growth of rural motorways in most parts of the Western World; the demand for them has been created by the rising tide of motor cars (world production of vehicles nearly doubled from 9 million to over 17 million vehicles per year between 1955 and 1965), whose makers and buyers have combined to bring heavy pressure to bear on governments to maintain, or even increase, their rates of road building. [5, 6, 7] As a result the faces of many countries have been transformed by very ambitious construction programmes. In a small island like Britain over 1,000 miles of motorway have been built in the last 13 years, and in the USA the figure is many times higher, with a 1965 total of over 41,000 miles of interstate freeways. A multiplier factor is at work, with new road construction encouraging increased use of private cars to the point where there is a demand for yet more roads to ease mounting congestion.

Increasingly heavy commercial and freight vehicles are also attempting to force their way into cities. In Western Europe, 40 ton juggernauts are common, and 59 ton lorries have trundled off ferries at Dover and Felixstowe on their way to destinations in England. Such monsters are completely destructive of the human scale of traditional cities.

Had the postwar motorway boom ended when it became apparent that existing cities could not accommodate the flows that they generated, little harm would have been done. What in fact was decided was to tear the cities apart to allow the traffic in. So-called link roads were built to motorway standards, sound housing was torn down, city districts dislocated, and the threat to the urban environment driven ever closer in towards the historic hearts of cities.

The recent traffic proposals for London provide a clear example of this tendency. The Greater London Council put forward a plan for a 25 year construction programme involving 180 miles of urban motorway (in three concentric rings or 'boxes'), estimated by the GLC to cost £1,400 million at 1969 prices (and by others as much as £2,500 million). [8] It would have necessitated the demolition of 20,000 to 40,000 dwellings, and caused the living conditions in many thousands more to deteriorate. By bringing motorway concentrations of traffic (of up to 12,000 vehicles per hour) to within 2 miles of St Paul's Cathedral the proposals would have flooded the existing road system with a volume of traffic that would have destroyed the existing environment, either by making normal pedestrian movement across canyons of traffic hazardous to the point of impossibility, or by tearing down existing buildings to blast an easier way for the traffic. Because the 30 miles of the innermost motorway, Ringway 1, would have contained 23 interchanges, 10 of them major ones with incoming radial motorways, large tracts of land would have had to be cleared to make way for miles of knotted concrete spaghetti, which would soon have become overloaded by the mass of traffic seeking to terminate its journey in the central 20 square miles of the metropolis.[9]

Instead of bringing about a much-needed reduction of vehicles in inner London, the proposals would have increased them by 40 per cent. The alternative policy of restricting private and encouraging public transport was not given a fair hearing, until the issue had become the subject of bitter public reaction.

A Transport Policy for the City
It seems likely that in the immediate future populations of Western countries will continue to rise, and that so will social interaction and interdependence. If urban motorways are not the answer to the problem of getting more people into and out of the cities, then some alternative solutions must be found which will not destroy city diversity, human scale and ultimately the very fabric. One sensible approach is to ensure that full use is made of existing central area roads by spreading the traffic load more evenly throughout the full 24 hours, and by prohibiting the use of circulation space for parking during the daytime. If wholesale and retail deliveries are confined to the 6 pm–8 am period, one major cause of daytime congestion is removed. The reduction of on-street parking places would in itself reduce traffic as well as increase road capacity, but this would have to be supported by severe restriction on the number of off-street car-parking places

in order to reduce the temptation to drive one's car to work instead of using public transport (which is six to ten times as efficient in its use of space). Techniques of road pricing for the innermost areas of cities (perhaps through an urban fuel tax or electronically triggered meters in cars) would add further teeth to such a policy.[10] The argument that this would discriminate against the poor ignores the fact that they would be the greatest beneficiaries from the resulting diversion of resources and custom from the private car to public transport.

This is the nub of the matter. Transport planning in cities must have two integrated aspects:

1. the control of the use of the private car;
2. the organisation of efficient and attractive public transport.

The process of preparing a traffic plan based on this strategy is logical and straightforward. Firstly, the places in a city which attract most traffic can be divided into two categories—those from which private cars should be as much as possible excluded (parks, pedestrian shopping areas, office complexes, and the city's central area) and those to which vehicular access is essential (industrial estates, docks and railway stations). A road system can be defined to link the main generators and attractors of traffic (places of residence and work) but avoid penetrating the safeguarded areas mentioned above, which should instead be provided with adjacent car parks, and bus and railway stations. 'Environmental Areas' of the sort with which Buchanan was concerned can then be designated and joined to the main traffic network, also ensuring that roads through districts in which safety or quiet is of prime importance are not used for through movement. When this basic road traffic and parking plan is integrated with the bus and rail systems, and the pattern of local centres, the skeleton of a transport plan emerges.

Far from damaging the commercial vitality of city and suburban centres from which cars are excluded, this type of policy brings new life to them. In Norwich, for instance, when London Street was pedestrianised in 1970, local shopkeepers feared loss of trade but in fact custom increased sharply. The same pattern occurred in the much larger and more ambitious Leeds scheme, where an area of nine or ten shopping streets covering more than 50 acres in the very heart of the town was closed to motor cars in 1971. Small buses circulate round the area picking up and putting down those who are not able, or do not wish, to walk. Apart from these vehicles, the only others allowed in are delivery vehicles, nosing their way through the throng of shoppers.

Stockholm's new suburbs of Farsta and Hogdalen encircle shopping centres designed to provide the same safe and pleasant pedestrian movement, with the added advantage of including underground railway stations, within the precinct, with fast and frequent links to neighbouring residential areas and to central Stockholm.[11] Vienna has gone to the lengths of banning all cars from the central area, in a large L-shaped zone of the inner city, which includes 704 businesses, most of the smartest shopping areas, and many of the best-known tourist sights.[12] The pedestrian zone extends for nine blocks, and will probably take in another five, including the State Opera House and the Cathedral as well as the shopping areas. Many businessmen whose premises are just outside the zone have now asked to be included. A local newspaper has commented that the innovation has 'spurred the Viennese to take possession of their inner city'. In a poll conducted by the city 80 per cent of those using the area expressed approval of the traffic ban. The main reasons given were cleaner air, less noise, better working conditions, and greater safety in the streets, Carbon-monoxide pollution levels in the area have more than halved.

Elsewhere, however, in New York, Birmingham, Los Angeles, Tokyo and Berlin, the motor lobby is still pressing its deadly concrete stilettos into the hearts of the defenceless cities. The production of motor cars is one of the basic sources of profit in the capitalist system of most Western countries, and every inch of urban land that is reclaimed from their domination will have to be fought for. In this battle between human values and machine men, logic is on the side of humanity, and we have the inspiration

of recent notable victories to give us heart. The most enthusiastic motorist is beginning to accept that the certainty of a parking
place, followed by a brisk walk or bus journey to his ultimate
destination, is better than a sticky search for a central-area parking place, fuming behind the wheel as he prowls around the car-
packed blocks ready to pounce on the first space that is vacated.
To such people the improvement of the environment may be a
little regarded bonus. To the everyday pedestrian, and the lover
of cities, it is salvation.

Avoiding Urban Thrombosis

Restriction of the use of the private motor car in city and suburban centres has the added advantage of diverting people back
to public transport, which is more socially acceptable in various
ways. It is available to those who cannot afford to buy or run
their own cars, or who are disqualified from driving by age or
infirmity; and it can move many more people in much smaller
channel space (a double-decker bus will take more than six
times as many passengers as the $2\frac{1}{2}$ cars which occupy the same
amount of road space—whether full or three-quarters empty).
Yet road and rail passenger figures are both falling year by year.
In Britain the number of bus-passenger miles alone has fallen
from a 1961 figure of 43,000 million by 25 per cent to only
34,000 million in 1970.[13] In the same period the number of
rail-passenger miles has fallen by 2,000 million, and a third of
the total length of railway line has been closed.[14] An increasing
proportion of a growing population has been diverted to the
socially wasteful private motor car, which has doubled its mileage
total between 1961 and 1970 to nearly 200,000 million miles,
over three-quarters of all travel in Britain. The most serious aspect
of this is that many of these switches have occurred in the journey
to work, when the roads are already at their most overloaded.

The urban transport crisis is often ascribed to the great affec-
tion which individuals develop for the personal comfort and
independence of the private car, but this is only part of the
explanation. Even more important is the paradox that once

society has provided roads and car parks, the motor car is at the same time the cheapest and least efficient of all forms of transport available to the individual; indeed, it is so inefficient that unaided it is incapable of handling the journey-to-work flows in any big city. If everyone who owned a car were to use it to drive to work in London, New York or Manchester, no one would ever get there.[15] On the other hand the immense numbers of workers converging on a single central area at the same time each day clearly suggests the need for special channels devoted to mass transit; these could be bus priority lanes or railway lines, fed perhaps by networks of more flexible transport facilities. Why then, as journey-to-work flows increase throughout the world, do existing railway systems find themselves driven to contraction, and sometimes closure?[16] The answer lies in the paradox that the massive organisation and investment which makes it possible for rail lines to bring 30,000 people into the centre of the city along a single track in one hour also makes them incapable of competing on equal economic terms with the private motor car. The latter is relatively cheap (its cost largely justified, to its owner, by its recreational and social use alone) and the upkeep of its track—the city roads—costs the individual no more whether or not he uses it.

By contrast, mass transit requires rolling stock, skilled operators and maintenance men, though the extent of their full use is confined to two periods of $1\frac{1}{2}$ hours each in the mornings and afternoons. Physical and technical obsolescence both set in rapidly, bringing the heavy cost of reinvestment. If interest-free loans are not available, price rises are necessary, and car owners switch to using their own vehicles, thus further damaging the competitiveness of the public-transport concern, with its fixed overheads. This is a classical case of what is beneficial for the group appearing unattractive to the individual, and what appears to be attractive to the individual being harmful to the group. In order that the greater good of society may prevail, the relative attractiveness to individuals of the two systems must be reversed. Public transport should be subsidised, in the same way as health and welfare, and the use of private cars in city centres during rush hours should be taxed.

A number of worried city administrations throughout the world have diverted investment from road to rail building, though few have acknowledged that the rail systems once built will still need to be continuously subsidised. San Francisco's celebrated Bay Area Transport System has cost over $2,000 million.[17] Its electric trains, computer-operated from a central station, will run at speeds up to 80 mph, with only 90 second intervals between trains at peak periods, making it possible to move 60,000 seated passengers an hour into the heart of the city, equivalent to 25 expressway lanes of cars. For a commuter living in a suburb across the bay the journey time to downtown San Francisco will be cut by two-thirds, taking only 15 minutes.

The US Department of Transport is sponsoring research into similar mass-transit schemes with futuristic names such as the Dashaveyor and the Gravitrain; on a larger scale new subsidised routes now link New York to Boston with the Turbo-liner (a high-speed experimental gas-turbine train); and to Washington with the Metroliner, an all-electric train which completes the 226 mile trip in 2½ hours at speeds similar to Britain's well-established inter-city expresses. John Volpe, Secretary for Transportation, has observed that:

> It has been proven that you are just not going to get the job done with highways alone. You can lay down a 12 lane express way and still not do the job. As a matter of fact what you do is just make more congestion. We can't tear down half our cities, and that is probably what you would end up doing if you tried to take on this job with highways alone. That's why I'll be fighting so hard for public transportation—because this is the way we've just got to travel.[18]

London, which has now rejected urban motorways through its inner areas, has recently opened its new £80 million Victoria Line, an addition to the network of underground railway lines that make repeated journeys around the metropolis cheap and easy, as well as helping with the rush-hour traffic. The Victoria Line was the first new rail line under central London for 60 years. The argument that the cost was now too great had been overtaken by the desperate need to keep pace with increased traffic. Experience of property values and social development on the Victoria Line has also shown that an underground can be an essential tool for stimulating change in the city.[19] Now the planners of London Transport Board have several new schemes under evaluation, and the Government has declared its intention of maintaining its present subsidy. Mass-transit rail schemes are being constructed or extended in Stockholm (where the building of new suburbs and railway lines are planned as single parts of the same exercise), Paris and Rotterdam. [20, 21, 22] Now that the average speed of travel in downtown New York has declined to 7 mph and in central London to 10-12 mph, transport other than the private car has become a necessity.[23]

It is not always necessary to go to the extremes of building new rail lines, or burrowing tunnels underground; for suburbs, and small and medium-sized towns, bus services may be dramatically improved if they are given priority lanes. This has recently been done in a medium-sized British town, Reading, which has a population of about 250,000. After a period of 5 years of continuous decline in the number of bus passengers, a system of five against-the-flow bus lanes and two bus-only streets was introduced in 1970. This resulted in buses passing through the city centre, cutting their running times by 2-5 minutes every trip, and in the service also being improved by the reduction in bunching. Numbers of passengers increased, thus reversing the previous trend for the town and the country as a whole. Despite a small increase, the fares are still the lowest in southern England, journeys of up to 1 mile costing 2p (or 5 cents), and up to $7\frac{1}{2}$ miles 5p (or 12 cents).[24] The concern is actually showing a profit, perhaps because the bus shares some of the inherent flexibility of the motor car, and demands much lower fixed overheads than the fixed-track systems like railways and monorails.

It is surely right to give public-service vehicles priority over motor cars in the competition for scarce road space. It may also be necessary to experiment with new systems of payment, or even subsidy. The British government has recently announced an experimental annual subsidy of £28 million for public transport—£8 million of it for bus services, most of which will go in matching grants to those local authorities who are willing to subsidise particular local routes out of the rates, on social grounds. In Sweden successful experiments have been conducted in abolishing traditional payment-per-journey fares, and replacing them with single monthly transport payments, equal to about £4 per month or 13p per day. This scheme has proved so successful in the small town of Halmstadt (where it prevented a further price rise, allowed the service to be improved, and increased the numbers of passengers) that it is now being introduced in Stockholm.[25] The monthly tickets give low-cost use of every public conveyance in the region, including ferries. The hope is that people will use them increasingly for shopping and weekend expeditions as well as to get to work. Bus lanes are to be increased two-hundred-fold, and bus-only precincts created. Pensioners, school children, and those on social security could be given free passes.

In Rome an experiment in completely free bus transport was enthusiastically taken up by many who normally drove to work, and resulted in reduced levels of congestion. The loss in fares, about £30,000 per day, was an increase of only 15 per cent in the normal operating loss.[26] Running the Rome bus system as a free public service would involve increasing the existing subsidy of £60 million per year by about another £10 million. In return, the pleasantness and convenience of the city centre would be immeasurably improved by a resulting reduction in the number of private cars; the historic environment would reappear from behind its present screen of exhaust fumes; buildings would be rediscovered as part of a network of urban spaces, instead of a series of facades appearing to float at a height of about 6 ft above ground level, over a constantly whirling conveyor-belt of cars.

Moving About The City

So far, we have been largely concerned with the regulation of traffic pouring into the city from outside. The other type of traffic, that moving from one part of the city to another, is also significant. If its demands are not met, the efficiency of the whole city will be seriously impaired. As we have seen, the city is essentially a meeting place, a centre of interaction, not only of producers and consumers but also of ideas, techniques, emotions, and experiences. Margaret Mead has called it the 'zone of confrontation'; for Jane Jacobs, one of its primary characteristics is its intensity; and there can be neither confrontation nor intensity without contact.[27]

There has been much theorising about the ways in which electronic communications (closed-circuit television, instant facsimile transmission, etc) will remove the need for face-to-face contact and cause the ultimate death of the city as we know it.[28] Such grand scenarios are oversimplifications. In the first place the steady increase of automation is shifting the emphasis of employment towards decision-taking and service jobs (because more routine ones are now being done by machines), and many decisions cannot be made on the basis of documented or transmitted evidence only. They must turn, in the last resort, on one's assessment of other people's reliability, judgement and honesty. It was this kind of consideration which caused the Dunning Report on the future of the City of London to reach the conclusion that while many routine jobs would leave the centre in the next 30 years, the numbers of people involved in jobs where face-to-face contact was necessary (commercial and professional services, the central cadres of government departments and higher education) would increase. The report concludes:

> Only those functions involving decision taking and close contact with people—clients, customers, or competitors—will remain in the Square Mile . . . The net result will be a labour force more highly skilled in expertise, judgement and experience, and land and buildings better utilized. The network of activities will be even more closely interwoven with each other.[29]

The point is that if the physical and social fabric of the area is so disrupted by having to cater for flows of vehicles generated elsewhere, its economic role, which depends on personal contact, will also be endangered. There are other reasons why the possibility of unimpeded contact must be safeguarded in cities; some of the most rewarding human activities need personal contact— one cannot make love by video-tape, or participate in a mass meeting by television. Attending a live performance of a play is very different from watching shadows move across a screen. Theatres, concert halls and pubs are of the essence of a city, as much as council chambers, clearing-houses, and hospitals.

Realisation of the importance of easy contact throughout the city led the brilliant mathematician and planning theorist Christopher Alexander to his famous observation that 'The city is not a tree' (using the word 'tree' in its mathematical sense as an hierarchical method of organisation); it was rather, he observed, a semi-lattice, in which people in any part might want to meet others in any other part without necessarily travelling into the centre and out again.[30] As employment is moving to the city's fringe, and new suburban shopping centres are opened, this is increasingly true; what are needed are new criss-cross public-transport routes in the inner areas, and outer ring roads taking the rural motorways round the edge of towns to their destinations, which may be the docks, industrial estates, public transport interchange points, or the next road intersection.

In order to ensure that the internal movement essential to the life of the city is protected and provided for, we must specify the various forms it may take.

Four main categories could be defined:

1. within local residential areas;
2. areas of repose and reflection;
3. central shopping and commercial areas;
4. between linked production processes.

New and existing residential areas can be planned to incorporate networks of safe and pleasant movement, with sequences of small spaces linked by footpaths to local shopping and service centres; movement of cars through living areas can be prevented by the placing of bollards at one end of streets, the space next to the bollards paved and provided with seats and perhaps a tree. Where pedestrian routes cross existing major roads, traffic lights and zebra crossings can act as bridges across the stream of vehicles. In this way not only will residents be allowed to re-possess their own environments, but spontaneous contact, the true key to neighbourliness, will be encouraged.

Most European and many American cities have inherited nume-rous areas of distinctive character and beauty. These include small parks, almshouse courtyards to which the public have a right of access, grand squares fronted by classically proportioned libraries and museums, the gardens of great houses which have been bequeathed to the city, cathedral closes, and peaceful tree-shaded churchyards. Too often the planners take such precious spaces for granted, and allow them to be isolated by heavy traffic, and reduced in scale by the construction of surrounding slabs and towers. In traditional cities, and well-planned modern ones, they form natural meeting and resting places, and it is essential that they be integrated into pedestrian-movement net-works.

At present the shopping and commercial cores of great cities are severely disrupted by the fumes, danger, and actual physical barriers created by the endless metallic processions of cars in the main streets seeking an escape route or somewhere to park. Jon Allison has pioneered an important new approach to demon-strating the inconvenience they cause to pedestrians.[31] He and his team recorded five different kinds of data in a busy area in central Nottingham: the size of pedestrian flows, the delays people experienced when their route was crossed by a road, how this varied with different levels of vehicular flow, the degree of overcrowding on pavements, and how this varied with space taken up for parking meters and traffic signs. Since the *average* waiting time at a crossing point was 31 seconds, and since the average number of crossing points which had to be negotiated by each individual was seven, a total waiting period of $3\frac{1}{2}$ minutes per person was involved in a single traverse of the shopping area of about ½ mile. This means that about a quarter of his time on the street was spent waiting to cross a road, subjected to a maximum of carbon-monoxide poisoning, and to high levels of noise. Since, in the last resort, city-centre shops and offices are trying to attract *people* (and only incidentally cars), it is foolhardy to subject central-area users to such appalling conditions. Allison observes:

> If the pedestrian interest is not sympathetically considered in city centres, then it is conceivable that the prosperity of those centres could be affected. We have heard for many years the argument that city centres must be accessible, that people must be able to get there, and, more controversially, park there. Clearly this is so. What has not been said either clearly or persistently is that once people get to the centre, they must be able to move about in it and use it to their satisfaction. People will tolerate inconvenience and discomfort, but there comes a time when the difficulties cause some groups to decide that it is not worth the trouble, that it is better to stay away. Among the first groups of people to cease making the journey to the centre are the old.[32]

As increasing proportions of the commercial activities of the city centre come to focus round face-to-face contact and exchange of expertise and information, the same considerations will increasingly apply to office complexes. Workers will want to be able to visit other nearby builldings for consultations without risking delays and danger. Exclusion of the private motor car from the commercial and shopping cores of cities and their replacement by small circulating buses would do much to improve their internal communications and to make them more pleasant and efficient. Terminal multi-storey or underground car parks could be located in the surrounding inner areas, attached to new public-transport stations.

It must not be forgotten that the city is still the centre of industrial innovation, and the nursery of new productive processes which, once established, can move out to larger, cheaper and less congested sites elsewhere. Within the small span of a few square miles the full range of industrial ingredients is available—manpower, banks capable of lending capital, technical consultants expert in special aspects, further-education institutions to produce particular skills, packaging and marketing concerns eager to handle new products, and, most important of all, small sub-contracting firms which exist by providing special components to other concerns. In one way the city is a marriage broker, making a good living by bringing eager partners together, and taking its fee in rates on their land. Contacts between them must be preserved. A small firm in, for instance, the South Docks area must be able to get its products without too much difficulty to the North East industrial estate. The main concern of such interconnected local firms is not that roads should run direct to all the sites with which they do business but that the town's roads should not be so full of cars on shopping or journey-to-work trips that there is no room left for commercial vehicles to fight their way out to a relatively clear ring road. The motorist who curses the big lorry easing out of a small entrance on to a busy road has exactly the wrong end of the stick—the lorry's path should be smoothed because it is contributing to the wealth of the community (and its load could not be diverted on to a different form of transport without damaging the city's economy), while the car driver could and should be travelling by public transport, or safely parked in a special space at the edge of the centre, instead of filtering round back streets in search of a stopping place.

Lest the discussion in this chapter conveys a sense of universal restrictions, controls and prohibitions, it should be pointed out that use of all the controls suggested would vastly improve the quality of the urban living environment while closing relatively small areas to private motor cars—perhaps 1 acre each in a number of suburban centres, and two or three areas of less than 100 acres each in city centres. Road pricing need only be applied in rush hours, so that at other times the highway would be free to rich and poor alike. And subsidies for public transport would return to the community very large benefits in terms of decreased costs elsewhere, increased social efficiency, greater social justice, and vastly greater enjoyment for all in our urban environment.

8 Cities and Towns

From their first development nearly 5,000 years ago, cities grew as the focal points of societies' activities and cultures, and these tended to determine their physical forms—the shape and arrangement of their buildings, paths, and spaces. The better the match, the more pleasant and efficient the cities tended to be. Where there was social and technical stability over a number of years, this balance between form and function often occurred naturally, through the steady replacement of jarring features. In times of rapid growth like our own, however, innovation outpaces adjustment, and harmonious settlement forms can only be achieved by conscious control. But much can be learnt from cities which have grown more slowly.

Form following Function
The relatively slow pace of social and technical change which was the rule until recently in many parts of West Africa gave rise to a number of such stable and distinctive settlements. Viewed on a map, these towns appear formless, mere jumbles of mud huts served by tracks of irregular widths; but closer observation shows them to be well organised and convenient, composed of sequences of dwelling, meeting and movement places, each suitable for its purpose. To appreciate them fully, one must discard the illusion that the geometrical products of machine processes

are inherently progressive, and therefore more aesthetically attractive than the irregular and distinctive objects and processes devised by individuals for their own use.

Some description of typical scenes in Onitsha Inland Town (which I happen to know well) may illustrate how appropriate town form may reflect and reinforce a people's culture. In the early morning activity is concentrated in the private spaces, within the high compound walls, shared by the several parts of one extended family; the air is filled with the smoky sweet smell of bitter leaf soup being heated over charcoal fires. As the sun climbs towards the vertical, shadows shorten, and townspeople move unhurriedly along the smooth red laterite paths, keeping close to the high walls of the neighbouring compounds, lingering in the shade of sacred trees, and hurrying by the small shrines of domestic deities, fearful of disturbing the spirits of the place and its people.

The shape of the track is constantly varied by widenings to form small and shady children's play spaces, and contractions to skirt the bases of particularly large and ancient trees. Here the foliage from two compounds may meet in a single vivid green arch, the cool circle being completed by a pool of shadow across the track. Passing through such an opening, the walker steps into a sun-drenched square, a heat haze shimmering inches above its baked red floor, and lapping against the 7ft high compound walls which form its edges. The tops of these are picked out in freshly applied whitewash, and some are decorated by large drawings of the clan's totem or sacred animal; tightly shut wooden gates, many intricately carved, reinforce the impression of security, permanence and privacy. Near the centre of the square under the shade of several huge trees is a small red and white shrine containing the sacred objects of the square's clan. This dominates the area, and it is impossible to enter the square, or move from one compound to another, without having one's attention drawn to it, and thus being reminded of the clan's unique history and traditions.

There are only three or four exits, and it is immediately evi-

dent in which direction each leads. As one moves through the
town, one passes through places with different symbolic associations—for example, the square of the leopard totem, and the
compounds round it belonging to the families of that clan; and
the Chief's square, entirely dominated by his high and ornately
painted compound wall and the huge carved gate in its centre.
Inside the compounds are shade, privacy and intensity, with many
small dwellings grouped round a central space; outside in the
public areas there are wide spaces, drama, variety and reminders
of the common heritage.

It must be stressed that such places are not charming relics of a
bygone age of tribal simplicity. Onitsha Inland Town is a vital
community accommodating over a quarter of the population of
one of Nigeria's great cities.[1] Most of the residents of the Inland
Town are wealthy traders and landowners who do their business
in the garish but modern river port. There they keep their cars
and their fleets of lorries; there are strong social as well as
physical sanctions against allowing these vehicles in to destroy
the historic environment of the old settlement. The Inland Town
is not an anachronism; it represents a successful continuation into
the twentieth century of traditional ways of living and organising
human relationships and spaces inherited from a past of many
centuries of organic growth. Its people are among the most
prosperous, well educated and influential in the city.

We can mould our towns to serve activities in the same direct
and sensitive way as Onitsha, but in our case the process must
be one of conscious planning rather than the slow eradication of
mistakes by trial and error over a number of generations. The
most important lesson is that the concern of civic design is not
the imposition of an abstract pattern upon a living community,
but the detailed matching of building and spaces to activities and
values, and the discovery of the ways in which one element can
be most naturally related to another.

Venice—an example of urban elegance
Venice offers a more dramatic, and larger-scale, example of the

same process as at Onitsha, made possible because the disruptive effects of the Industrial Revolution have been excluded by the saving grace of its location on mudbanks of limited size in the Adriatic.[2] If there is no space for factories, neither is there any room for cars, because the city is built as a dense network of fine classically styled dwellings, interlaced by the canals whose thin bonds keep Venice as a city of the Adriatic as much as of the mainland. The only road is that which runs along the 3 mile viaduct to Mestre on the mainland, and terminates at the edge of the city. The visual grandeur of Venice was created by the wealth and pride of its merchants and sailors, bringing back from their trading and plundering expeditions oriental ideas and oriental wealth that went into the construction of the ostentatious splendour of St Mark's Cathedral, with its huge dome and richly carved façade rising straight from the tesselated paving of the famous square. But had Venice been on the mainland, not all the city's wealth could have prevented the square being turned into a dual carriageway and car park; the cathedral's vista being blocked and blackened and its structure shaken by incessant battering by traffic for fourteen hours every day; and the slim finger of the Campanile dwarfed by gleaming towers of steel and glass.

Venice is in a vulnerable environment in which there has been little place for modern technology, and the happy result has been the preservation of a city truly human in its scale and character. One of the first things one notices while moving about it is its quietness; the only sound is the intermittent, distant putt-putting of the water buses on the main canals. By contrast, the squares which punctuate and focus the dense network of dwellings, passages, and canals, seem far livelier than the average British or American high street. Because the visitor's ears are not closed to exclude the roar of traffic, he hears a constant vibrant symphony made up by many human voices—greeting, arguing, bargaining, and rejoicing. It is significant that in a city devoid of many of the elements that are normally regarded as the most dramatic in modern life, such as motor cars, skyscrapers, and massive urban redevelopment schemes, the quality of drama should be so constantly present. Each square is like a stage, and the dense network of dwellings around it the wings, full of fascinating characters about to emerge to perform a scene whose script is 700 years old but which has never been enacted in exactly this way before. The real drama of towns is a human, not a technological, one, and it can only be properly performed and enjoyed where the stage is built on the human scale.

Amsterdam—a planned city

In many ways Amsterdam, reclaimed from the mudbanks of the old Zuyder Zee, is a similar case, though its development over the past four centuries has been marked by far more conscious planning than that of either Onitsha or Venice. The city was itself created by an act of planning—the draining of the marshes by cutting canals which also served as routeways and defensive barriers. As the city grew outwards, concentric rings of new canals were built, crossed at right-angles by radial roads running from the dam at the centre of the city. The Building Ordinance of 1565 stipulated that all piling foundations of dwellings should be approved by municipal officers before building could begin, that each plot should have its own privy, and that streets and paths should be paid for by those whose dwellings fronted them but be constructed by council employees.[3] Under another sixteenth-century regulation, all dwellings had to have a frontage of not less than 26 ft on to a canal or a street and be separated by a minimum distance of 160 ft from the backs of other dwellings.

It is not just the splendid tree-lined pattern of wide and elegant canals reflecting the old Dutch and classical fronts of the tall buildings, and the varied structure of the many bridges, which give Amsterdam its unique urban character; it is also the generous size of private gardens close to the city centre, and the repeated pattern of façades, trees, canals and bridges. As in Onitsha and in Venice, it is the appropriateness of the basic unit for the activities they must perform—dwelling, movement, exchange, meeting, or simply contemplating—that decides the visual and emotional quality of the city. If the physical form is true to the activities and values of the people it serves, then it will also be readily understood and memorised by them.

Thinking Big and Feeling Small

The three examples quoted share a common characteristic: their pattern was determined by the human activities performed within them, and by the details of the local environment; their social scale reflects the human scale. Modern city dwellers know that this is no longer so. Their urban environments are being revolutionised by developments in constructional technology which have made buildings 200 ft high a common feature, and by a similar change in the scale of thinking of those who are responsible for urban design—planners, architects and developers. Such people constantly exhort each other to 'think big' and scoff at the traditional design virtues of restraint, simplicity and harmony. If Ebenezer Howard laid in front of society his gentle dream of the garden city as a reaction against the massive scale of the industrial city, Le Corbusier's vision of the Radiant City which still pervades much urban design was conceived as a gesture of industrial man's independence and defiance of traditional constraints. Making maximum use of new techniques became a virtue in itself; the production of alien environments was justified on the grounds that by living in them people would learn to raise their standards till they preferred them to traditional buildings; height of structure became synonymous with adventurousness of design. Other architects, such as Mies Van der Rohe, began consciously to seek for an anonymity in their buildings that would match the mood of a mass-production society.[4] We are increasingly now living in their world—a world of cosmopolitan architecture of excessive scale, formality and repetitiousness. The problem is at its worst in city centres, where high land values and pressure for redevelopment present a ready-made justification for the destruction of vivid and humane environments and their replacement by vast impersonal structures.

London's Victoria Street, a windy canyon walled mainly by

vast slabs of concrete and glass offices, occupied at street level by glass- and plastic-fronted shops, is a typical case in point. The street is wide but because of the great height of the structures on either side it appears narrow; heavy traffic pours along the carriageway, which is normally dark and heavily shaded; pedestrians hurry, heads down against the channelled wind, along the dead-straight pavements. To be in Victoria Street means to be going somewhere else; to want to be somewhere else. Down the Thames, on the south side, the inner-city 'New Town' of Thamesmead, built on an area of reclaimed marshes by the Architects Department of the Greater London Council, is similar. Many approaches could have been adopted: designing to meet the housing objectives of the client groups; borrowing from successful models on similar sites such as Amsterdam; re-creating recent popular British housing developments, such as terraces of town housing; or experimenting with other men's inspired schemes, such as Safdie's Habitat. Instead they chose an arid and formal pattern of vast and bleak structures which channel the cold north-east wind so well that children and old people have been repeatedly blown off their feet. [5, 6]

Planning for oppression

Few British or American cities are without their own examples of Radiant City planning: Manchester (England) has pioneered avenues of twelve-, fourteen- and sixteen-storey tower blocks along the main radial routes out of the city to the north, Jersey City (New Jersey) has a tangle of unrelated and jostling downtown office blocks, and Philadelphia has its vast new civic and commercial centre. Such features are uniquely the products of a machine age; their form has been determined by machines and the materials available, rather than by any human considerations.

A South African geographer once remarked of the modern township of Sharpeville, built by the white government to house the black miners of the Witwatersrand, that its full elegance could only really be appreciated from the air. Viewed from ground level it was apt to seem dull, repetitive and tawdry; on a lesser scale the same is true of much perfunctory planning by members of the elite for the rest of society. Intricate city-centre movement patterns, and delicate arrangements of informal spaces, are swept away to be replaced by geometrical and rigid channels, edges and walls. For the resident, the result is a sense of alienation from his own environment; for the stranger, that sense of disorientation which is becoming familiar to most travellers.

If the arrangement of many new city-centre developments is composed with a drawing-board formality that totally ignores human perceptions, the sheer size of many of their structures is humiliating and frightening; in an environment composed of blocks so vastly out of proportion with our own scale, our aesthetic reaction can be either to submit or to rage. In such an unnatural setting natural emotions are distorted: love of one's fellow human beings is curdled to hatred of the buildings in whose shadows, and along whose corridors, they are forced to scurry; the pleasure of pausing to greet friends or exchange salutations is replaced by a restless feeling that one must keep moving to meet the pressures of urban life; instead of a sense of possession of the city, we have the feeling of being owned by it. The physical impact of these structures—giant office complexes, shopping and hotel precincts, and vast urban motorways—is equally serious. Wind is channelled off their blank faces into the narrow conduits reserved for movement, and across the empty plateaux from which they rise. The huge concentrations of workers or shoppers which they accommodate come flooding along roads thrown like javelins into what was once the living heart of the city.

The materials necessary to such a scale of building are also alien—huge walls of concrete, steel and glass, over which the eye slides looking in vain for some familiar element with which it can associate. (The use of traditional brick not only gives a façade pattern and diversity but also reminds us subconsciously of its composition from large numbers of units, each of which can be held in the human hand.) What symbolism there is heightens this

aura of strangeness: the landmarked focus of the square and
statue, or fountain, is replaced by an abstract and illegible concrete bas-relief on the towering end-wall of a new office block.
The celebration of beauty or civic pride is replaced by a monument to big business. But in the main the old images which gave
meaning and a sense of continuity to our cities are being destroyed
without the creation of any alternatives. Each cycle of urban
redevelopment destroys more of the unique and historic
reminders of our culture, such as old almshouses, guildhalls,
Victorian covered markets, historic buildings and, perhaps most
important of all, humane street patterns which developed in
response to the movement needs of pedestrians of roughly the
same size and shape as those who have used them ever since.

Competing panaceas

In this matter, as with all others concerned with the planning of
societies, no progress can be made without reference to the city's
present or future residents. For many centuries civic design was
in the hands of dominating elites who developed successive,
rather arbitrary concepts to mirror their own particular values.
The regimentation and inequality of early Mesopotamian,
Indian, Egyptian and Roman civilisations was well expressed in
the strict gridiron patterning of their streets, and their frequent
recourse to vast monumental features. Ancient Greece, with its
delight in intellectual experimentation, produced more artistic
groupings of buildings, including many, such as the central part
of Athens, the Acropolis, the Temple of Delphi, and Hippodamus'
city of Piraeus, which are still regarded as perfect models by some
civic-design experts.[7] European medieval towns, growing up
within the fabric of surrounding feudal conservatism, seem to us
to exemplify a more organic form, which is also very attractive to
some modern theorists.[8] In many ways these towns were similar
to the example of Onitsha.

The return to the learning of the ancients in Renaissance times
brought with it a renewed classicism of form which was developed
by later absolute monarchs into the extravagant grandiosity of

the baroque princely city.[9] In one way, the industrial city—
nineteenth-century Manchester, early twentieth-century Chicago
—could be seen as a functional approach to town planning,
though of course only from the viewpoint of the entrepreneurs,
who took good care to live outside them.[10] The romanticism of
thinkers like Camillo Sitte represented an almost predictable
reaction against such a subjugation of aesthetics to profit.[11] Today
all these schools of thought—classical, organic, baroque,
romantic, and a number of different types of functionalism—
are forcefully expounded by competing champions. Their views
have become grand abstractions and analogies, useful only for
the teaching of the history of urban design. If we are to develop
our own philosophy and principles of civic design, we must see
that they mirror the social values and political organisation of
our society just as those of former ages did theirs. In Britain and
the USA, society is a formal democracy with strong overtones of
oligarchical plutocracy. It is one of the themes of this book that
since the democrats decry what they see as plutocracy, and those
accused of being plutocrats vociferously affirm their allegiance to
democracy (and their willingness to spend their last drop of
money in its defence), we have no logical alternative but to use
the criterion of democratic theory as the touchstone of our
design.

City Form and City Image

Such an approach to civic design has been pioneered by Dr
Kevin Lynch of Harvard, and is described in detail in his
important book *The Image of the City*.[12] Lynch's starting point
is that a person's view of his environment is subjective, in that
it is the area of which he has a mental image, a form of map
within the mind. Such a map is necessary if he is to find his
way easily and agreeably about his daily business. It will be
initially composed of a series of disjointed fragments, which
should be capable of being linked together to form first sequences,
and later a unified network, within which he can locate any point
or place within the city. Thus the rather vague word 'image'

acquires a new significance: it is the mental code which permits us to understand, memorise, master and enjoy our environment to the full. Knowledge of how such images are formed, and of which patterns of structures and spaces give rise to clear and pleasant ones, and which to confused and unpleasant ones, thus becomes valuable.

In order to help in understanding this, Lynch devised three original types of survey. The first consisted of intensive office interviews, each lasting $1\frac{1}{2}$-2 hours, with about 100 local residents specially selected for their perceptiveness and articulateness. The aim was to discover which elements and features of the city they found most memorable, what emotions they associated with different places and vistas, and which features they used as reference points in their journeys through the city. Secondly, these results were checked by asking the same questions of a random sample of people stopped in the street. (In fact the differences were only ones of greater detail in the longer office interviews.) Thirdly, a system of urban classification was developed, using features found to be significant in the earlier surveys; and intensive field surveys of the areas were carried out by trained staff to find out why interviewees had found certain features and districts more pleasant and memorable than others.

How we know where we are

The conclusions were as interesting as the methods. City features were perceived as being of one of five major types—paths, nodes (focal points), landmarks, districts and edges. Routes that passed through areas of distinctive character were preferred to more direct but less varied ones. The most popular were those along which there were activities of changing intensity, or progression past a series of identifiable landmarks, so that the traveller was constantly aware of getting somewhere. Landmarks themselves were remembered as much for contrast, prettiness, symbolism or colour as for sheer size. The fact that the Medical Centre in Jersey City has a small landscaped plot in front of it seems to be as important an identifying characteristic as its great

bulk and skyline silhouette.[13] Nodes such as small squares, intersection points and pocket parks were valued more for their
emotional and symbolic attributes than for specific physical ones.
A good British example of this is London's Piccadilly Circus with
its statue of Eros.

Lynch's interviewees associated districts with interesting
activities and unusual types of topography. Boston's Beacon Hill
is a classic case, being steep, old, affluent, well maintained and
full of beautiful buildings. London's Chelsea, Paris's Montmartre
and New York's Greenwich Village all possess a similar
'imageability', which localities such as Stuyvesant Heights and
London's Barbican High Rise Flat scheme entirely lack.

Clearly defined edges may reinforce the mental map of the
city, particularly where they mark the end of a district, as they
do along waterfronts or at the beginning of an industrial area;
too often, however, they are great slashes through the middle of
living districts, like urban motorways or the hard and intrusive
modernity of a new educational precinct. They become dividers,
where they should link activities on both sides unifying the use,
and image, of the whole city.

Lynch argues that the main aim of civic design should be to
make the city legible to its residents, and to offer them repeated
pleasant perceptions. By implication he rejects the high rhetoric
of traditional approaches as being irrelevant to, and uncon-
cerned with, the dilemmas of modern urban society—classicism's
preoccupation with regimented and geometrical patterns to
suppress the natural diversity of an individualistic civilisation,
the restless search of romanticism for the picturesque, the
repeated descent of organic design into mere whimsy, and the
persistent failure of the functionalists to define which functions
are most important, and in whose interests they are planning.

In the light of his work Lynch advocates that cities should
prepare plans for their future visual form based on people's
actual perceptions. A large sample of the population, balanced
to match the general population characteristics, should be asked to
do four things:

1. draw a quick sketch-map of the area in question showing the most interesting and important features and giving a stranger enough knowledge to move about without too much difficulty;
2. make a similar sketch-map of the route and events along one or two imaginary trips, chosen to represent the length and breadth of the area;
3. make a written list of the parts of the city felt to be most distinctive, the examiner explaining the meaning of the words 'parts' and 'distinctive';
4. put down brief answers to a few questions of the type 'where is .... located?'[14]

From this information a visual map of the city as it is experienced by a statistically valid cross-section of the residents could be composed, showing which areas are well connected and which confusing; where existing character should be preserved and where enhanced. If reactions to different existing structures and parts of the city were also recorded, it should be possible to design new buildings that would add to the environment instead of destroying it, as at present. The town planner and architect who may feel uneasy about such destruction of a subtle and intimate environment and its replacement by a gigantic and domineering one has nothing to offer against the enthusiasm of the developer now but his own intuition. Armed with the type of future visual-form map which Lynch advocates, he would be able to use traditional development-control techniques to ensure that all new buildings either respect existing visual patterns, or help to create attractive new ones where they are now lacking.

It is lack of such a positive policy for the appearance and structure of existing cities that makes development control so negative. Its greatest triumphs are no more than rearguard actions preventing a proposed office block from rising to a height where it would dwarf an existing attractive skyline, or insisting on the stepping back of a high building from the street line. If designers were in a position to tell developers what type of new urban feature they wished to see in different parts of the city, vitality and interest might be added to the townscape by new development instead of being steadily destroyed, as at present. Small but significant open spaces and patches of decorative gardens, for instance, could be added at strategic points as part of the agreement to permit new development.

In the physical design of new communities, too, the starting points should be the satisfaction of the residents, and efficiency in satisfying their wants. At the moment efficiency tends to be calculated only in terms of achieving minimum initial construction costs, and satisfaction is assumed on the basis of 'What these people *really* want is . . . . (insert in the blank space 'privacy', 'community', 'modern design', 'space' or 'garages' according to taste and fashion).

The return to the criteria of emotional satisfaction and psychological security which Lynch's consultative approach offers us is important not only for its technical simplicity, but also because its effect would be to throw the quality of life of the individual citizen into the balance against the financial advantages of building concerns and investment companies. The existence of a visual-form map for all city centres, and all areas where development is proposed would act as a check against the irresponsible and as an invaluable guide to the many architects who regret their part in the dehumanisation of our urban heritage.

In the absence of this kind of information there is a real danger that designers will be tempted towards a spurious originality, like Corbusier's disciple Oscar Niemeyer in the high-rise concrete wilderness of Brasilia,[15] or the Greater London Council architects in the windswept wasteland of Thamesmead. Those who talk about building new environments for new epochs forget that changes in man's technology have not significantly altered his stature, the level at which he views the world, the structure of his mind, the ways in which he gains his pleasures, or the images with which he associates them. New Towns should offer their first occupants more, not less, of the visual pleasures that they derived from their former environments. The reason that Venice,

Amsterdam, Siena, Agades, Kandy and a dozen other well-known focal points of international tourist traffic offer the resident and the visitor alike such superb aesthetic rewards is not that in some past golden age their designers discovered some secret principles; they grew up slowly, so that each addition had to respect what already existed, and could be envisaged as a part of the whole. We must repeat the entire process of defining the forms and arrangements which satisfy and are memorable to us, and design, as they did, to please ourselves.

9 Quantity and Quality

All planning must be concerned with both quality and quantity—not only what we want but how much of it and how distributed. There is no human activity which does not require a careful balancing of these two issues. We need, for instance, food of a certain quality of nutrition and tastiness, and we also need enough of it to satisfy hunger. If some have too much, others will have too little; the health of the one group will be damaged by excess, while many in the other will be condemned to a premature death through deficiency. Similarly it is not enough that the houses and schools we build are efficient and elegant; they must be in sufficient number to meet the needs of all. Otherwise the pursuit of one set of qualities will lead us to violate another—justice.

The problem is particularly acute in Western countries because of the widening gap between the world of technology (which is by definition concerned with increasing the quantity of output) and the world of the humanities (which deals with values to which it is difficult to ascribe numbers).[1] Because of the highly specialised nature of the two activities, this division was, until recently, more often defined than bridged. Extreme technological determinists proclaimed that human values were no more than a by-product of their own activities, and they advocated 'social engineering', to condition modern mass societies to a state of docility—'beyond dignity and freedom', in the phrase of B. F. Skinner.[2] Concern for quality, on the other hand, has too often degenerated into attempts at preserving the privileged position of 'cultured' minorities rather than fulfilling the hopes for better lives of the rest of society. Influential writers like T. S. Eliot have treated the word 'values' as if it was synonomous with 'minority values', and the word 'culture' as though it were solely an attribute of the elite.[3, 4]

The Elitist Approach

The advantages to the nation of supporting small cliques of highly paid trend-setters must depend upon a rapid dissemination of new benefits to all classes; but this is precisely what elites, once they have been allowed to form, do all they can to prevent, sending their children to separate schools, living in separate areas, and accentuating different characteristics of speech and manner that can effectively exclude non-members from the privileges of the charmed circle. The idea that God-given subjugation to higher authority is itself spiritually beneficial is also untenable. When the saintly Mr Wilberforce (who owned factories but not slaves) pleaded that reduction of the working hours of children under the age of eleven in factories and mines to 10 hours a day would be but the first step on a dangerous descent to godlessness, he was asserting that *his* view of what was good for the working classes was the right one.[5]

A further argument is that society must concentrate material, educational and cultural resources where they are most needed, and that this is in the nurture, training and support of highly qualified experts and decision-takers, who will draw the national chariot forward at a spanking pace, thus contributing to the well-being of all. This argument has always been fallacious, since cities are inherently collections of interdependent specialists. We toss the remains of the child's dinner in the dustbin, and only the conscientious work of the dustman stands between us and typhoid. We flick a switch and light floods our room, illuminating well-loved books, themselves the priceless gifts of earlier specialists, many now dead. Whole trains of work by vast numbers of our fellow citizens make possible this casual but recurrent miracle; miners hewing in cramped conditions half a mile underground; railway workers piloting their steel monsters through the black silence of the night; men in the power stations maintaining constant vigil over their furnaces and turbines; the copper miners of Rhodesia and Chile, precision engineers in a dozen different industries. Within the nation (and with the possible exception of stockbrokers) there is no significant group whose activities are not vital to the continued well-being of us all. The argument that the doctor is more important, and should be paid more, than the dustman is not only wrong but irrelevant. The one is concerned with prevention of disease, the other with its cure, and both are indispensable.

The association of quality with scarcity is false. Quality is the product of careful and specific design. The gay and chic mass-produced clothes of young people today are far more attractive and appropriate to their purpose of decoration than were the heavy and expensive tweeds of Britain's 'county set'. Much mass-produced china, glass, and wood ware is of the highest quality. Just as one tree does not lose its beauty through being one among millions, so can dwellings, shops and sports facilities cater for the mass demands of society without sacrificing quality. Low quality is the product not of a mass market but of the concentration of power in the hands of a contemptuous elite.

The Sacrifice of Quality

It is not surprising that the opposite obsession with growth (constantly producing more of everything) should be even more widespread at the present time. The increasing scale of modern mass society is dramatically illustrated by the fact that the average population of the world's 190 odd nations is nearly 20 million persons each and that four nations each have populations each in excess of 200 millions.[6] The very organisation and administration of such huge states demand further developments of the mass-production and communication systems which fostered their original growth. Great resources and attention must be devoted to the basic questions of dealing with large numbers. Nevertheless, we must not forget the inherent dangers of dehumanisation which could lead to the sacrifice of those very qualities which make life worth living.

The use of the computer symbolises this knife-edge problem of dealing with large numbers without losing sight of human values. In many of its useful operations it is an ethically neutral tool; such activities as the calculation and printing of pay slips for large organisations, computing of tax, and recording and storage of medical data do not have inherently sinister implications for the life-styles of those involved. In other sectors, such as the processing of research data, there may even be occasions when computers can improve the sensitivity and effectiveness of society's response to human problems by matching the vast numbers of people concerned with a means of automatic data handling that helps in reaching conclusions. Dangers arise when decisions based on value judgements affecting other people begin to be taken by those operating the computers. Increasingly in both the USA and Britain administrators may hand over an entire issue or problem to systems analysts or operations researchers, and accept their conclusions somewhat uncritically.[7] This is particularly true of transport problems and questions of land-use planning. The workers who write the programme on which the computer will base its analysis have no alternative but to make the crucial value-judgement themselves; this may give rise to the notorious 'Gigo Effect' (Garbage In—Garbage Out).

The analysts are only too aware that every 'objective' they have to incorporate in their programme represents a further constraint that will more or less double the amount of calculations that will have to be done (because a computer works by checking every factor, however obviously irrelevant to a human brain, in a straight yes/no way); they do not pester the politicians for too many such constraints, both because they wish to get out an answer quickly and because they know each additional one will increase the already enormous expense of the operation.[8] The computer also needs very simple value judgements, because the addition of weightings further complicates the calculation process. The final result is a solution produced at two removes from the original problem, on drastically simplified criteria, geared towards values largely invented by the person who designed the programme. These values will be so deeply embedded in the whole calculation process that it will not be possible for the non-expert to identify or question them.

The reaction of the individual citizen, aware that his problems are not being solved, and that he is incapable of affecting the process by which decisions are being reached, often becomes one of frustration, resentment and ultimately alienation. Roger McGough's poem *M 66* expresses this:

The politicians,
(who are buying huge cars with hobnailed
    wheels the size of merry-go-rounds)
have a new plan.
They are going to
put cobbles
in our eyesockets
and pebbles
in our navels
and fill us up
with asphalt
and lay us
side by side
so that we can take a more active part
in the road
to destruction.[9]

The sense of violation of fragile human flesh by dead materials, the perception of 'planning' as both arbitrary and gimcrack, the sense of regimentation of individuals, the impression of 'participation' as a deceitful mockery, and the ultimate association of the whole process with deathliness, sum up the citizen's feelings. The perception of impersonal forces as being inherently threatening is inevitable; because they are so much larger than ourselves that we cannot turn them aside, and because they are composed of statistics rather than the human values with which we are familiar, we often cannot understand them, predict how they will behave, or take evasive action, until it is too late. To redress this situation, the entire process whereby large-scale plans are prepared must be geared to identifying and expressing the qualities which the people affected most seek in their lives; and there must be abundant points of personal and public scrutiny to ensure that the qualities the plan is striving towards do not go through any mysterious changes in their passage from public consultation to permanent structures.

We have already seen one classical case of the erosion of quality by the pursuit of quantity in the tower-block syndrome.

Admirable as has been Britain's concern for rehousing those in bad accommodation in the last quarter of a century compared with, for instance, the USA, there has often been an unfortunate obsession with numbers. Successive Ministers have pledged themselves to particular numerical targets. The result has been that the normal client-contractor relationship has been severed. 'Housing units' have been slapped up anywhere, and very often anyhow, and the first and last say that their prospective occupiers have had is when they have said 'yes' or 'no' to the offer of the tenancy.

Prophesying by numbers

Confronted with trend projections of world population growth which they are incapable of putting into a realistic geographic context, a number of architectural gurus have flung off their professional garments and plunged into the seductive waters of technological prophesy, half in panic, half in ecstasy. Thus Buckminster Fuller offers us his vast space-enclosing 'geodesic domes'—which he describes as:

> Delicate fireproof pre-stressed concrete open-framework tetrahedral cities consisting of hundreds or even thousands of decks . . . on which the floatable, flyable, roadable mobile-home mechanical containers will be economically parked as their occupants dwell locally for periods during their world-round peregrinations.[10]

It is not exactly that the endearing Fuller lacks concern for quality in his desire for the maximum fulfilment of every single human being. He possesses a real regard for the quality of life; the problem is that he is a superb technician first and a poor philosopher second. As a result he always treats quality as if it were a simple by-product of quantity. For him, an object is totally defined by its dimensions, which is why his attempt to glorify man takes the form of building vaster cities. Because he does not regard qualities as having an independent existence, it does not occur to him to check if the quality of life inside his geodesic dome will be what people want. (To me it sounds like a recipe for universal nervous breakdown.)

Other seers of undoubted originality like Paolo Soleri, disciple of Frank Lloyd Wright and founder of the Cosanti Foundation, offer similar comphrehensive solutions. Soleri aims at the creation of a 'multi-level human ecology', and proposes 'gigantic beehive-like structures to house vast populations at densities of well over 600 people to the acre'.[11] Constantin Doxiadis who runs the world's largest town-planning consultancy service from his 'Athens Centre for Ekistics' (ekistics being roughly translatable as the science of the best use of space), and who awards his own degrees to his own students in a subject which is his private property,[12] has spent his career in pursuing quantity. The inevitable growth of Dynapolis (a sectoral growth diagram which Doxiadis has elevated into a universal urban solution) must lead to the formation of a linear world city (called Ecumenopolis) constantly getting itself knotted in areas of high population density. The Athens Centre for Ekistics (ACE) offers to supply vision at reasonable rates, but totally in terms of technique, scale and quantity. Because his ideas are value-free and concerned only with number, his ekisticians can happily produce plans for any political system. They are universally acceptable to any power structure because they seek to change nothing. Though devoid of quality, they provide a physical structure capable of accommodating the greatest possible amount of growth, and thus bring closer the advent of Ecumenopolis—a world city of, surely, shattering inequality, repetitiveness and banality. Consultation is not on his agenda.

Trash for Profit

We are all so familiar now with the cycle of the mass production of trash that it is perhaps too easy a target. Children get new plastic dolls every month and throw away the bits. The phenomenon of induced obsolescence, first identified in the USA by Veblen in the late nineteenth century, was widely accepted until recently as being a legitimate part of automobile manufacture.[13] It took years of research and court actions by Ralph Nader, author of *Unsafe at any Speed,* to make car manufacturers acknowledge even so basic a quality as safety in their products. If we made better cars, levels of output could be reduced, work satisfaction increased and consumption of non-renewable resources diminished. Recent research by Frank Costin, a Bedfordshire specialist car-builder, has shown that wood is light and stiff, and with properties of low deterioration, good energy absorption, and freedom from mechanical fatigue. More important, the trees felled for this purpose could be replaced in a way which metals cannot, and would not confront society with the same disposal problems as do metal cars. With thought, we should be able to raise not only the quality of our products, but also that of the environment, which too often in the past has been despoiled to create them.

Quality and quantity can and must be brought into balance. Realisation of this is increasing in Japan, which has experienced the most rapid rate of economic growth of any nation in the last 25 years. Along with rapidly rising output, exports and consumption, have gone mounting tides of urban and industrial refuse, and the world's worst pollution problem.[14] Now the government and business leaders have agreed that the goals of the economy must be predominantly qualitative rather than quantitative, to balance the developments of the recent 'economic miracle'.[15] It is suggested that social-welfare improvements must take precedence over production increases and that foreign-exchange earnings must be used rather than hoarded. The economic-planning agency is even proposing to develop a new yardstick of national economic health, the Index of Net National Welfare, to replace gross national product. This would take into account such things as environmental disruption and general living standards, as well as increases in the output of goods and services. This turning back from the edge of the precipice is particularly interesting because Japan had advanced further and faster along the road of sacrificing values to output, quality to quantity, and people to products than any other nation. If she shows the same efficiency in her return as she did in her flight, the rest of the world may be presented with an admirable example to follow.

It is as wrong to assume that we are concerned mainly to meet the demands of x million units of consumption, as that our primary aim should be to create a limited number of exquisite items of permanent artistic value to cater for the elevated tastes of a small elite, leaving the rest of us to make do with what we can get hold of. Not only the numbers but the characteristics of people's wants must be measured. The waste-production factor (which periodically floods society with a worthless new novelty, or produces goods with intentionally short lives) must be reduced; and that diversity which is the hallmark of culture must be preserved. There is no doubt that this vision of a society constantly reviewing its own nature and needs and seeing that they are met in ways that will cause as little disruption as possible in the harmonious relation between man and man, and man and environment, will appeal to many; it may be regarded by some as utopian. The difficulty in its fulfilment lies in securing honest and effective consultation; its greatest strength lies in the argument that consultation is a self-reinforcing process. The act of consultation makes people think more deeply about their values and aspirations; it leads on in some cases to a greater insistence on power sharing, and to the stimulation of a desire for participation, first in local affairs and then in matters affecting the whole nation. Such an attitude is an important safeguard to prevent democracy dying of sleeping sickness.

Participating in Local Affairs

It has already been stressed that participation and consultation are not interchangeable terms. Participation means sharing power; consultation means being asked one's preferences before decisions are taken. Participation can be seen as the safeguard of quality, because if people directly affected by a new development share in deciding where and what it will be, and how it will be run, they will insist on high standards. But such participation inherently involves small numbers of residents' representatives, who, though in touch with local opinion, do not possess an infallible sense of the priorities and needs of the much wider numbers who make up the whole community; and they may not even be in sympathy with those that they are aware of. In order to ensure that these quantity considerations are acknowledged, some form of consultation will be necessary. It may be as informal as members of a residents' association talking to their acquaintances in their daily round of shopping and working; or it could be as formal as a scientifically conducted 100 per cent attitudes survey. In the same way that quality and quantity must be balanced to achieve satisfactory social results, so must participation by local leaders be balanced by consultation with a wider range of local residents, if the re-emergence of an opinionated local elite taking decisions on behalf of large numbers of other local residents is to be avoided.

This process of consulting can all too easily be used as a smokescreen to hide the fact that decisions have been taken much earlier. Such an approach—termed 'talk therapy' by Sherry Arnstein, the American planning theorist—forms one of the lowest rungs of her 'ladder of participation.'[16] However, since residents and amenity groups may also ignore other local opinions with which they disagree, some form of safeguard is needed for all concerned. This can be provided by joint oversight of consultation by municipal officials and representatives of local groups, so that neither side can afford to cheat, and the resulting information is equally available to both. Criticism of the present practice of consultation in the USA (Mrs Arnstein describes it as 'tokenism') is based on the observation that at the moment local people 'lack the power to insure that they will be heeded by the powerful'. The frustration which she describes on the part of residents subjected to repeated 'attitude surveys' stems from their having become suspicious of the choice of questions and impatient of the lack of action resulting from previous ones.

There are two particularly interesting aspects in Mrs Arnstein's approach. The first is her distrust of the good faith of existing planning agencies. For her, a return to traditional methods can only mean continued exclusion of local people. She cites numerous examples of manipulation and tokenism in New Haven, Philadelphia, Providence and other places, in the operation of some parts of the recently wound-up 'Model Cities' programme, and only sees progress being made where partnership, delegated power, or full citizen control results in local people actually getting their hands on federal money, dictating how it should be spent, and hiring and firing their own technicians. In other parts of the Housing and Urban Development departments' programmes the introduction of 'City Demonstration Agencies' committed to local control has allowed such a thoroughgoing delegation of power.

In Cambridge, Massachusetts, for instance, the City Demonstration Agency (which had complete control over the programme) was composed of 16 elected residents' representatives and only 8 appointed by public and private agencies.[17] The fact that under federal statute the final power of endorsement still rested with the city council was a recognition of the rights of the representatives of the whole city's ratepayers to vet proposals for spending public money, and did not detract from the genuine gaining of planning initiative by local people. A further democratic control was provided by the requirement for all such proposals to be approved by a neighbourhood referendum. This reversal of the normal situation, whereby city officials prepare plans which are then subject (at least in Britain) to objection by local people, seems entirely logical. It is similar to that already described (page 62), whereby the Greater Paris Council has delegated its planning powers for the redevelopment of the Les Halles area to a residents' committee.[18]

While such an emphasis on real power is universally valid, it is significant that it should stem from American theorists. Planning in the USA has traditionally followed financial objectives of increasing property and rateable values, and aesthetic ones of achieving a modernistic environment, in contrast to the predominantly social origins of British town planning with its preoccupation with slum clearance, new towns, and provision of open space and social amenities.[19, 20] It is not only that British planning has often been qualitatively better than American planning; it is also that the criticism of local people has been more often directed against the means it has used than the goals themselves. There is less deep-seated conviction that the planners are 'on the other side' than there is in the USA. Though they may have been seen as remote, bureaucratic, high-handed, unimaginative, even authoritarian, up until recently there has been little conviction that British planners were the tools of big business[21] The disillusion of leaders of the minority groups in America's inner cities is expressed by Carmichael and Hamilton, writing in 1967:

> Urban renewal and highway clearance programmes have forced black people more and more into congested pockets of the inner city. Since suburban zoning laws have kept out low income housing, and the Federal Government has failed to pass open occupancy laws, black people are forced to stay in the deteriorating ghettos. The crowding increases, and slum conditions worsen.[22]

Professor Nathan Glazer's account of this failure of American redevelopment programmes to acknowledge the special problems of the poor and less competitive has already been cited (page 40).[23] He shows how the urban-redevelopment machine is controlled by big business, and is not only insensitive but hostile to the interests of the present occupants of the inner city. Consultation has been discredited by persistent misuse; if it is to regain its credibility it will have to be channelled through the medium of participatory residents' organisations.

There are good reasons why such a breakdown of trust is unfortunate. There are many large city-wide issues (such as spending priorities and environmental preferences) for which local groups will not be the most appropriate bodies to test opinion, both because their findings will frequently conflict with each other, and because the implications of proposals (such as the construction of a new mass-transit system) are experienced on both a city and a local scale. It seems eminently desirable that cities should have development (or 'structure') plans to prevent repetition of the unregulated, unpleasant and insanitary pattern of nineteenth-century urban growth, and that such plans should reflect the priorities of the majority of the city's residents, and also cater for as wide as possible a proportion of minority interests. Inside this general structure plan there must be considerable flexibility, and its component parts must be under continuous review as a result of *participation* in the development process by local groups. One or two examples of why a structure plan is necessary may be helpful here.

Lack of it tends to give rise to the kind of 'disjointed incrementalism' which incorporates every new technological innovation into the urban fabric irrespective of its impact on the existing city.[24] For example, the preparation of such a plan would involve the asking of questions as to the relative importance attached to housing, transport and environmental improvement, so that the numbers of new urban motorways, if any, that should be built could be decided, as well as the proportion of public money that could be spared for subsidising public transport. There would also be questions on the kinds of densities and environments that people prefer, and whether they were willing to pay more in construction costs for the 'benefits' of high-rise living. Other issues that would have to be considered would be the balance of new civic investment between maintaining the dominance of the existing commercial centre or encouraging the growth of new suburban ones.

These are questions which can be answered from the individual's own experience. One possible technique is the 'priorities

listing' (page 91) used by Young and Willmott.[25] Another
approach is to ask specific questions, such as the following:

> How long would you be prepared to spend travelling to your
> daily and weekly shopping.
> What features do you most value in your present district?
> What features do you most dislike in your present district?
> Would you like to leave this district?
> What features would you most value in a new house?
> What do you think is the ideal place for children to play?

The greatest problem about using this kind of consultation as the
basis for future plans lies in ensuring that the questions are
framed, and the answers processed, honestly. Otherwise, local
authorities will simply finish with the numbers and the features
they had first thought of.

It is for this kind of reason that the then President of the Royal
Town Planning Institute, F. J. C. Amos, made a plea in 1972
for more citizen-planning advocates to come forward to oppose
the work of the official planners, and keep it under constant
review: 'It is these groups who are most in need of help, and who
are the cause of so much social concern. They should have
their cause effectively argued and pressed'.[26] But it is not
only opposition, but also openness that is necessary. In Liverpool, where Mr Amos was planning officer, work is beginning on the preparation of a structure plan for the new Metropolitan Authority of Merseyside, which will have a population of over 2 million people. A metropolitan-wide priorities
sample survey is being conducted at an early stage, using intensive publicity in the local press. If local residents' associations are
contacted to give advice on the framing of the questions, and in
stimulating local interest, the necessary degree of public scrutiny
and involvement may be generated.

It is hard to see how genuine *participation* of local groups
could be made effective in the preparation of such a large-scale
and generalised plan; their most effective role is to make sure
that the consultation process is conducted honestly, and that its

results do not merely get microfilmed, filed and forgotton while the officials get on with the serious business of guessing the future. If it is on questions of specific developments and management that participation is most effective, it is on ones of objectives and spending priorities on which consultation has most to offer. It should not be disregarded because it has, in the past, been abused. The principle of consulting the client is an old and sound one. Where the client has 2 million different faces and sets of experiences, the process *must* involve statistical processing, but if this is kept under adequate supervision it need not involve falsifying the results.

The ladder of participation

The other particularly interesting aspect of Mrs Arnstein's approach is her underlying optimism that citizens, having been initially fobbed off with manipulation, 'therapy' or one or another form of mere tokenism, will learn to demand more genuine levels of participation, and to insist that public programmes be made more relevant to their needs and responsive to their priorities. They can climb the ladder of participation. Even manipulation has a value, since, as we all know, being duped is a most effective form of education. The mere supply of information leads on to questioning of established ways of doing things; and the very invitation to consult creates questions about how honestly the findings are being used, and stimulates an insistence that one be taken into partnership in decision-making. Finally the whole idea of the expert with particular qualifications and rights to make decisions about how the rest of society should be organised can be challenged, thus reducing technicians to their proper advisory role.

Allied to rising standards of education throughout the world, and increasing periods of leisure time in post-industrial societies, the demand for local people to have a greater share in decisions affecting them must accelerate. Realisation of this trend is leading governments throughout the Western World to propose more consultation, with consumers, customers and citizens.[27] The resulting organisations, such as community councils, the British Gas and Electricity Boards Consultative Committees and Transport Users' Consultative Committees, may often be seen as little more than public relations exercises, siphoning off complaints in a safely harmless direction.[28] Nevertheless, the habit of complaining is deeply ingrained in both the British and American characters, and the mere existence of a body to receive the complaints encourages people to effective protest. And once the citizen has made his first complaint about an official body his foot is firmly on the first rung of the ladder of participation. There is no guarantee that 10 years later he will automatically be found exercising full citizen control over the matter about which he complained, or sitting on a committee with delegated powers; an ingenious officialdom can protect its powers, culminating in a simple refusal to relinquish them. But in a democratic society administrative reforms will follow, though tardily, on public pressure, and the official's room for manoeuvre will be constantly diminished.

The 5 year dispute over the location of the proposed third London Airport illustrates the mounting difficulty experienced by bureaucrats and national-level executives in steamrollering through their plans by using the inexorable justification of their own expertise. In 1966 Peter Masefield, then chief executive of the British Airports Authority, stated that London was in desperate need of a third airport if dangerous levels of congestion at Heathrow and Gatwick were to be avoided; he thought that delays in approval by the Board of Trade (the government department concerned) could result in serious consequences for safety and for the future of Britain's competitive position in world air transport. Stansted, site of a largely disused American air base, was said to be the best location. The then President of the Board of Trade speedily decided that he must follow the advice of his experts, despite an outcry from nearby residents and permission was given for Stansted to be developed. The protests of local people were echoed by transport theorists outside government and public-administration academics who were appalled at the arbitrary way in which such an important decision had been taken.[29] After months of stonewalling, a new President of the Board of Trade announced that as the new airport would cost several thousand million pounds, and could possibly affect the lives of hundreds of thousands of people, a Royal Commission would be appointed to select and evaluate a number of alternative sites, including, if they so decided, Stansted.

In fact the Commission decided to select a short list of sites on the criteria of accessibility, interference with existing airports, and nuisance caused to existing communities. Stansted, which only months previously had been categorically stated by experts to be the *only* suitable site, was not one of the four selected for evaluation. These consisted of three inland sites and one coastal one. Largely due to the high valuation placed on passengers' time (£5.55 an hour at 1968 levels) relative to that placed on the 'costs' of the nuisance caused by noise to nearby residents, one of the inland sites, Cublington, emerged from the cost-benefit analysis as being the best value.[30] By this time public opinion was thoroughly sceptical of all expert advice on the matter, and the outcry over the selection of Cublington exceeded, if anything, that which had greeted the choice of Stanstead 4 years previously. The protests had succeeded in one respect: the issue had been thrown firmly back where it should have been in the first place, on a politician's desk, where it could be influenced by consultation with the people most likely to be affected. As a result, the site which emerged from the cost-benefit analysis as the worst value of the four, the coastal one at Foulness, now re-named Maplin Sands, was finally chosen by the government. One interesting sideline on the affair is that during the delay generated by the debate, public scrutiny was directed to the fundamental question of whether an extra airport was really needed, bearing in mind the increased passenger-carrying capacity of the new wide-bodied aircraft, and the lesser runway space required by planned short take-off planes. These doubts surfaced in the Civil Aviation Authority's *Survey of Air Traffic and Capacity in the London Area,* published early in 1973, which indicated that

the need was not for new runways but for new passenger ter-
minals, which could be adequately provided at existing airports.
Despite these recommendations, the government announced its
intentions of persevering with the Maplin proposals. In the face
of the inevitable public outcry, however, they may be no more
successful in this than in their commitment to the Stansted site.
Whatever is the outcome of the Malpin issue, the result of the previous rounds was a victory for an oddly assorted alliance of residents' groups, academics, politicians and amenity associations
which had together mounted the ladder of participation very
quickly (in 7 years) from despairing protest, through formal consultation by the Royal Commission, to militant opposition and
ultimate success. Each such victory enlarges the credibility of citizen power, and acts as a lever moving the centre of gravity of the
decision-making process a few inches further away from anonymous experts and towards the people who will be most affected.

Community action

Community action is not simply a mushroom growth of the last
few years. We have seen (page 42) that its roots in Britain go
back to the seventeenth century, with the brave attempt of Winstanley and the Diggers to create an alternative and egalitarian
society. The establishment of cooperative communities on both
sides of the Atlantic by Robert Owen and his son in the early
nineteenth century gave impetus to a movement in both Britain
and America that, though often dormant for long periods, has
never been extinguished. Its reappearance in the twentieth-
century United States occurred dramatically in the mid-thirties
in the Back of the Yards district of Chicago, one of the most
notorious parts of the Western World's most notorious city, in
the middle of its years of gangsterism and depression. Saul Alinsky,
a sociologist and activist, joined forces with a local clergyman and
park director to organise a carefully structured district council
under the slogan 'We the People will work out our own destiny'.[31]
The council soon came to exercise many of the functions of local
government that had gone by default in the area for many years.

Policies were set by a kind of legislature of 200 elected representatives from smaller organisations and street neighbourhoods. As wartime and postwar full employment solved the worst problems of poverty, local residents found themselves faced with the familiar alternatives of staying in bad accommodation in an area in which they had grown up (and developed valued patterns of association) and moving out to unfamiliar but more sanitary suburbs. The dilemma was posed in a particularly acute form by the blacklisting of Back of the Yards for improvement loans by mortgage companies.

In 1953, the council approached financial institutions in which local people had large deposits, and forced a reversal of this policy. Within 3 years some 5,000 houses had been rehabilitated. Nobody had been thrown out of the district and relocated, and no business had been destroyed. The district had identified and solved its own problems by community action.

Such an approach is today no longer uncommon. In 1972 a residents' association in Cardiff won the first recorded victory of local people against the cuckoo encroachment of rapidly growing universities, when, after a prolonged campaign, a Department of the Environment inspector ruled that the university rather than the residents should be moved out of the central area, on the grounds that this

> would reduce the need to clear areas of reasonably good housing in or near to the centre, and would avoid the destruction of established communities. Severe hardship would be inflicted on the considerable number of people, many of whom are old and infirm, who would otherwise be displaced. Some of them are too old to start living somewhere else.[32]

The opposite battle was fought in Newcastle upon Tyne. There the Planning Department decided at the beginning of the 1960s that Rye Hill, an area of 15 streets of large, once upper middle-class, Victorian houses should not be demolished but 'revitalised'. It took this decision without public consultation and indeed without even making a specific survey of the condition of the dilapidated and often horribly multi-occupied houses until 1967. When the council got round to doing a few pilot modernisations in 1968, the cost for one of the smaller well maintained five-room houses was £3,300. John Taylor, who was involved in the situation from the beginning describes what happened:

> The residents were overwhelmingly against the scheme. The council was forced to concede some consultation through an advisory committee of street representatives, but the council took the autocratic view that public participation meant 'You, the people, participate in *our* plans.' When, at a public meeting at the end of 1967, the people decisively rejected these plans, the council simply abolished the advisory committee. Jon Gower Davies has pungently documented the whole fiasco in his book *The Evangelistic Bureaucrat.*
>
> The reasons why people rejected revitalisation fell into two groups. The owner-occupiers and long established tenants who dominated the Rye Hill Residents' Association (formed 1966) opposed it because it was being applied with a rigidity that meant that owners would lose their houses if they could not afford to bring them up to the council's high standards. Their main concern was to get themselves excluded from the scheme.
>
> The tenants in turn had no confidence in the plan, since earlier council modernisations in the district had been damp and defective. They felt they were being cheated of new houses, and anyway most wanted to be out of a notorious and insalubrious area. So a group of us formed in 1967 the West End *Tenants' Association*. We argued that most of the houses had deteriorated so far that either revitalisation would be no cheaper than new housing and would produce high rents; or if the Council tried to economise on revitalisation the people would not have homes fit to live in.
>
> A good policy (the improvement of old houses) was being misapplied, and earning itself a bad name because of an authoritarian approach which did not think first to consult before imposing a cherished solution. In fact in 1968 the Ministry of Housing scotched this scheme too, on the grounds that it constituted an abuse of compulsory purchase powers. The Council has now cleared and is redeveloping the centre of the area and is proceeding with revitalisation, in only half the fifteen streets.
>
> The West End Tenants' Association have kept a close watch on the progress of revitalisation. In 1972 we carried out a survey into the condition of modernised houses in the western end of the area. Despite the high claims, we found that out of 102 tenants 68 complained of dampness, 63 complained of ill-fitting doors or windows, 46 complained of plumbing faults etc., etc. Forty-four tenants said that overall they were satisfied with their homes, compared with 56 who said they were not. Two were undecided. [See *Evening Chronicle*, Newcastle, 23 February 1972]. Newcastle Council responded with denials, denunciations and threats of legal action, but they are in fact conceding our allegations by sending in repairmen to put matters right. The architect himself now admits that major items were wrongly installed.[33]

In London's Piccadilly another developers' fantasy has run into such a welter of public protest, professional criticism and political embarrassment that it has had to be withdrawn. It would have involved the demolition of the existing dense network of theatres, cinemas, clubs and restaurants which make Piccadilly Circus the entertainment-focus of the country, and the construction of over 500,000 sq ft of new office space (despite the fact that there are already four skyscraper office blocks within $\frac{1}{2}$ mile of the circus which have been vacant for a number of years, and that it is government policy to restrict the further growth of office employment in central London).[34] The scheme is almost a caricature of the kind of city-centre concrete heart transplant discussed in Chapter 5, with all its unneeded offices being suspended over a traffic causeway that would have drawn in enough vehicles to ensure a devastation of the surrounding areas similar to that of Piccadilly Circus itself.[35] The chairman of the 'Save Piccadilly' campaign observes that such development is 'dictated by greed and not by need'.[36] Responding to public outcry the Secretary of State has called in the application, and the scheme has been drastically amended, with office space being reduced and pedestrian areas at ground level greatly increased.

Protest and prevention

Although there have been occasions when individuals within the power structure have been forced to acknowledge the right of people on the receiving end to participate in decisions affecting their areas, citizen participation is mainly expressed as a mounting tide of international dissent. All over the world citizens' groups are stopping things that they don't like. In Toronto and San Francisco urban motorways have been stopped short in their tracks and in the latter city proposals to build two skyscrapers respectively 840 ft and 550 ft high at focal points in the city put into abeyance.[37] In Tokyo plans to turn one of the islands in the bay into a giant refuse tip have also been amended.[38] In London three years of resolute opposition by local groups has resulted in the scrapping of plans for the construction of 80 miles

of urban motorway; in the same city the Golborne Community
Council has not only won its battle to save one of its districts
from being slum-cleared, but has gained acceptance of participation of the existing residents in planning the resulting improvement scheme.[39] The route of Liverpool's proposed M62 motorway
into the city has been diverted along a railway line and away
from private housing after consultation with local residents'
groups. In the historic cities of York and Bath destructive tunnel
and road proposals are being effectively challenged by local
amenity groups.[40] Recently New York citizens' groups have succeeded in killing a proposal for a new state motorway which
would have devastated their areas for the benefit of out-of-town
motorists.[41]

Such successes depend not only on the ability of groups to
band together, and gain strength from unity, but also on the
courage and determination of individuals like Saul Alinsky,
George Clark and John Taylor. Without their resolve much community action would have no starting point. Even the isolated
individual can be enormously effective. For example, the Russian
engineer and Nobel Prize winning novelist, Alexander Solzhenitsyn, who has survived Stalin's prison camps and the effects of
stomach cancer, continues to direct a stream of well argued and
cool criticisms at the excesses committed against individuals by
the police state which he refuses to leave. Not only does he dare
to write upbraiding the head of the KGB for the behaviour of the
secret police; he even smuggles the text of his letter out of the
country for publication in the West.

> For many years I have borne in silence the lawlessness of your
> employees: the inspection of all my correspondence, and the confis-
> cation of half of it; the search of my correspondents' homes, and
> their official and administrative persecution; the spying around my
> house; the shadowing of visitors; the tapping of telephone con-
> versations; the drilling of holes in the ceiling; the placing of re-
> cording apparatus in my city apartment and garden plot, and a
> persistent slander campaign against me from speakers' platforms
> . . . (As a result of this attack against my friend) I can no longer
> remain silent.[42]

Perhaps the most extraordinary feature of this letter is the result it achieved; Solzhenitsyn received an official apology for the beating-up of the friend for whose sake he was complaining. Pete Seager, imprisoned by the United States government for refusal to turn informer against former communist associates during the McCarthy purges of the 1950s, has not received this courtesy, but the two men are of the same stamp. All the organisations in the world would not produce effective movements without the inspiration of a Bertrand Russell, a Jean-Paul Sartre, a Mahatma Gandhi, a Ralph Nader, or a Martin Luther King; and sometimes where protest *groups* cannot be organised at all only the isolated voice of an Alexander Solzhenitsyn or a Pastor Niemoller is left to keep alive the truth that government and plans should exist to serve the people.

Notes and References

1 THE URBAN PARADOX (pp 9–22)

1 Davis, Kingsley. 'The Urbanization of the Human Population' in *Cities*, a *Scientific American* book (New York 1965, reprinted London 1967), 18–21
2 Davis, 15 (graph)
3 Davis, 21–4
4 Strong, Josiah. *The Twentieth Century City* (New York 1898); and Steffens, Lincoln. *The Shame of Our Cities*
5 Census of Population, 1971
6 *Local Government Bill* (1972). The proposed boundaries separate cities from their hinterlands, and indivisible functions such as planning and social welfare are shared between district and county authorities
7 Wherever basic grievances of poverty and inequality cannot be solved peacefully in cities, there is a danger of violence. Recent examples are in Reggio Calabria (*Guardian*, 'Reggio's revolt brings results', 16 March 1972) and Montevideo (*Guardian*, 'Tupamaros eliminate a death squad', 21 April 1972)
8 Thomson, David. *England in the Nineteenth Century* (1950, reprinted 1961), 134. 'In 1865–6, a further outbreak of cholera forced the issue . . . in 1869, a further Commission drew up a statement of the "basic conditions necessary for a civilized social life"'
9 Lindsay, John. *The City* (1971)
10 Weber, Max. *The City* (1904, reprinted New York 1966), 94
11 Le Corbusier. *City of Tomorrow* first published as *Urbanisme* (Paris 1924). Translated and reprinted (London 1947). Also *The Radiant City*, first published as *La Ville Radieuse* (Boulogne 1925). Translated and reprinted (New York 1967). Le Corbusier advocates that all activities should be accommodated in very high buildings supported on pillars, set in landscaped parkland, and joined by very fast motorways.

176

12 Richards, J. M. *Modern Architecture* (1940, reprinted 1962), 50–2
13 'Collapse of Newsham Tower Flats', *New Society* (1968), 295. The Ronan Point Tower Block collapsed in May 1968, probably because progressive collapse of its component panels was triggered by a minor gas explosion in one flat. Five people were killed.
14 Jackson, Harold. 'New Yorkers face $141M tax increase' (*Guardian*, 19 April 1972)
15 Davidoff, Paul and Linda, and Gold, N. N. 'Suburban Action: Advocate Planning for an Open Society', *Journal of American Institute of Planners* (Jan 1970), 13. Between 1950 and 1966 the population of the USA's suburban rings increased by four times as much as that of the central cities. Eli Ginzburg points out in *Manpower Strategy for Metropolis* (New York 1968) that in the 1950s New York lost 837,000 whites and gained 727,000 Negroes and Porto Ricans.
16 Abrams, Charles in *Cities*, a *Scientific American* Book, 141
17 Glazer, Nathan in *Cities*, 196
18 Friedman, J. 'The Concept of the Planning Region', *Regional Development and Planning, A Reader*, ed Friedman and Alonso (Cambridge, Mass, 1964), 512–15
19 Lindsay, 201–6
20 Hansen, N. 'Regional Planning in France', *Journal of the American Institute of Planners* (Nov 1969)
21 *Report of the Royal Commission on the Organization of Local Government*, Cmnd 4040 (1969)
22 *Local Government in England, Government Proposals for Reorganization*, Cmnd 4584
23 cf A. H. Marshall. *New Revenues for Local Government*, Fabian Research Series, 295 (1971), and *The Future Shape of Local Government Finance*, Cmnd 4731 (1971)
24 Leach, S. M., Heywood, P. R., and others. *The Zone of Transition*, an unpublished study of three areas in Manchester (1968)
25 *Report of the Committee on Housing in Greater London*, Cmnd 2605 (1964)

2 THE SOCIAL IMPACT OF TECHNOLOGICAL CHANGE (pp 23–35)

1 Webber. M. 'The Urban Place, and the Non Place Urban Realm', *Explorations into Urban Structure* (Philadelphia 1964). McLuhan, M. *Understanding Media* (1964, reprinted 1967). Meier, R. L. *A Communications Theory of Urban Growth* (Cambridge, Mass, 1966)
2 McLuhan, Marshall. *The Gutenburg Galaxy* (1962, reprinted 1967)
3 McLuhan, Marshall, *Understanding Media* (1964, reprinted 1967), 7–9 and 348–50
4 *Removing Lead from Gasoline*, Mobil Computer and Management Science Division (New York 1971). Report quoted in *Sunday Times* 'Oil firm admits lead danger in petrol', (5 September 1971)
5 Three distinct viewpoints are becoming apparent on this topic:
   1. A thoroughgoing advocacy of economic growth and increased consumption on the basis that technology will produce new

resources to replace those that are now being consumed. See W. W. Rostow's *The Stages of Economic Growth* (1960)

2. An entirely opposite view is adopted by Paul and Anne Ehrlich. *Population, Resources, Environment* (1970), who argue that *maintenance* of living standards and a continued increase in population would involve consumption of non-renewable resources that would leave the world uninhabitable by the end of the century.

3. In contrast to these growth and restriction philosophies Professor Barry Commoner in *The Closing Circle* (1972) believes that what is wrong is the *misuse* of technology, and he argues in favour of 'environmentally compatible technologies', imposed on industry by governments in the interests of society. His concern is to reintroduce a stable relationship between *each* individual and his resource base, rather than to reduce demand by compulsory cutting back on population.

6 Harris, Anthony. 'Taxes "take" dropped but poor got poorer', *Guardian* (12 January 1973), quoting from *Economic Trends* explains 'In 1971 . . . the poor continued to get relatively poorer and the rich slightly richer . . because changes in tax and benefits failed to keep up with the tendency for the high paid to gain proportionately more than the low'.

7 The USA's Conservation and Peace Corps, and the UK's International Voluntary Service, Voluntary Service Overseas, Young Volunteer Movement, and Inland Waterways Association are all examples. Mayor Lindsay claims that in New York 25,000 young volunteers have involved themselves with the work of the city's Urban Action Task Force, during school, college, and university vacations. Lindsay, John. *The City* (1969), 125

8 Lord Rothschild. *A Framework for Government Research and Development* (1972). See also Anthony Tucker. 'Rothschild Unacceptable' and 'Chairman's Plan for Research', *Guardian* (2 February 1972)

9 Tucker—'Green for Protest, White for Hope', *Guardian* (1 May 1972)

10 Illich, Ivan. 'The Politics of Conviviality', a BBC Radio 3 Broadcast, 11 December 1971, argues in favour of restricting extreme developments of 'High Technology' in favour of 'Intermediate Technologies', which will be of more benefit to more people. This is also the theme of Schumacher's book *Small is Beautiful: Economics as if People Mattered* (1973)

11 Harris, Amelia. *Labour Mobility in Great Britain, 1953–63*, Government Social Survey (1965), 9, Table 7

12 Getze, George. 'Additive to and DDT's dangers', *Guardian* (14 July 1971), reprinted from *Los Angeles Times*

13 Tuohy, W. 'Fight to save Mediterranean', *Guardian* (29 Feb 1972) quotes French underseas explorer Jaques Cousteau that 'Today you can hardly see a fish three inches long', and Swiss Marine scientist Jacques Piccard that life within the sea will be dead within 25 years unless society acts quickly. See also Commoner, Barry. *The Closing Circle* (New York 1972)

3 *PLANNING AND THE POWER STRUCTURE* (pp 36–51)

1 Mills, C. Wright. *The Power Elite* (1956) and Sampson, Anthony. *The Anatomy of Britain Today* (1965)
2 Schon, D. *Beyond the Stable State* (1971), Chapter 2 'Dynamic Conservatism'
3 Mill commented of mid-nineteenth century British government: 'There is in fact no recognised principle by which the propriety or impropriety of government interference is customarily tested. People decide according to their own personal preference'. 'On Liberty', *Selected Writings of John Stuart Mill* (New York 1968), 128
4 Mill, 130–2
5 Mill, 160–4
6 'Plea for more roads', *Guardian* (Jan 1972) summarises the special pleading of a British Road Federation pamphlet *Finance and Roads*
7 Jackson, K. 'Participation in Community Development', *Challenge*, Liverpool Education Committee (March 1970)
8 Lindsay, John. *The City* (New York 1969, reprinted London 1971)
9 Bacon, Edmund N. *Form, Design and the City* (1962), a film strip
10 Glazer, Nathan. 'The Renewal of Cities', *Cities*, a *Scientific American* Book (1967), 191–3
11 Jacobs, Jane. *The Death and Life of Great American Cities* (New York 1961, reprinted London 1965)
12 Glazer, 194
13 Maher, Chrissy. '£17,000,000 to Spare? Liverpool the Real Priorities', *Community Action* (Feb 1972)
14 'The Real Cost of the Civic Centre', *Liverpool Free Press* 3 (1971)
15 Woodcock, George. *Anarchism* (New York 1962, reprinted London 1963), 22–6. Winstanley was a prolific and cogent pamphleteer; in his pamphlet *Truth Lifting Up Its Head Above Scandals* he established the philosophical basis of his movement as a rationalistic one:

> Let reason rule the man, and he dare not trespass against his fellow creatures, but will do as he would be done unto. For reason tells him is thy neighbour hungry and naked today, do thou feed and clothe him, it may be thy case tomorrow and then he will be ready to help thee

16 Plumb, J. H. *England in the Eighteenth Century* (1950, reprinted 1960), 82
17 Thompson, David. *England in the Eighteenth Century* (1950, reprinted 1961), 45
18 Radford, J. 'Squatting Prospects', *New Society*, No 409 (30 July 1970)
19 Grapevine. 'Speaking Hypothetically', *New Society*, No 425 (19 Nov 1970) and Grapevine. 'Southwark Sequel', *New Society*, No 428 (10 Dec 1970)
20 Skeffington. A. M., Chairman of Committee on Public Participation in Planning. *People and Planning* (1969), 1
21 Skeffington, 47, Recommendation IV

22 *Town and Country Planning Act* (1968), 4 (sec 3), 7–8 (sec 7)
23 Morton, Jane. 'In Defence of ATACC', *New Society*, No 441 (11 March 1971)
24 Young, Michael. *The Role of Neighbourhood Councils in a Reformed Local Government*, Institute of Community Studies, cyclostyled report (1972)
25 Hillman, Judy. 'State Aid for Road Noise Victims', *The Guardian* (4 Feb 1972)
26 Wilson, Des. 'Minority Report. The Facts Heath Wouldn't Reveal', *The Observer* (27 Feb 1972)
27 Whitaker, Ben. *Participation and Poverty*, Fabian Research Pamphlet No 272 (1968), 2–8
28 Arnstein, Sherry. 'The Ladder of Participation', *Journal of the Association of American Planners* (July 1969, reprinted in *Journal of the Town Planning Institute*, 57, No 4, 1971), 177
29 Arnstein, 180–2
30 Marcus, Susanna. 'Planners—who are you?' *Journal of the Town Planning Institute*, 57, No 2 (1971), 55
31 Marcus, 59
32 Mills. *The Power Elite*, 225 41
33 Heywood, P. 'Plangloss, a Critique of Permissive Planning', *Town Planning Review*, 40, No 3 (1969), 257–8
34 Mumford, Lewis. *The City in History* (New York 1961, reprinted London 1969), 514–28
35 Paul and Linda Davidoff, and N. N. Gold, 'Suburban Action: Advocate Planning for an Open Society', *Journal of the American Institute of Planners* (Jan 1970)
36 Coates, K. and Silburn, R. in *Poverty, the Forgotten Englishman* (1970)
37 See, for instance, the new bi-monthly magazine *Community Action*, available from 9 Pattison Road, London, NW2

4 WHAT VALUES? WHOSE OBJECTIVES? (pp 52–71)

1 Le Corbusier. *The City of Tomorrow* (1929, reprinted 1947). Published as *Urbanisme* (Paris 1924) and *The Radiant City* (New York 1967). Published as *La Ville Radieuse* (Boulogne 1925)
2 More. Thomas. *Utopia* (1516 Latin edition, 1556 first English edition, reprinted 1967)
3 Mannheim, Karl. *Ideology and Utopia* (1929) and *Man and Society* (1936). For short summary see Floud, Jean. 'Mannheim', *Founding Fathers of Social Science* (1969)
4 *Management in Local Government*, Vol 3, *The Local Government Elector* (1967), 43
5 Hill, 94; quoting from *Management in Local Government*, Vol 3, *The Local Government Elector*, 16, 53
6 According to *Management in Local Government*, Vol 3, *The Local Government Elector*, councillors spend on average 7½ hours a month on local problems; nearly a third had seen fewer than one elector a week in the month preceding the survey (226–8).

7 Examples are Sheffield's deck access housing schemes at Hyde Park and Park Hill, London's comprehensive education system, and the pioneering work done by the Chatham (Kent) Council in establishing wardened homes for the elderly.

8 Morton, Jane. 'In Defence of ATACC', *New Society*, No 441, (11 March 1971)

9 Mumford, Lewis. *The City in History*, 416–20

10 See also, for example, the TCPA's weekly *Planning Bulletin*, as well as such as major publications on special topics as O. W. Roskill's report *Housing in Britain* (1965). A similar role to the TCPA is performed in the USA by the admirable Regional Plan Association.

11 *People and Planning*, Report of the Committee on Public Participation in Planning (1969) 66, Appendix 8

12 Alexander, Christopher. *Notes on the Synthesis of Form* (Cambridge, Mass, 1964) develops an entirely logical and practicable means of doing this.

13 An urban poll held on this topic in Manchester in 1968 achieved only a 2 per cent vote in the city as a whole.

14 A friend in the Department of the Environment believes that this section to be unfair on the grounds that consultation is being encouraged in General Improvement Areas, through a £200,000 publicity campaign.

15 'Covent Garden', *Community Action*, No 1 (1972), 12

16 Windsor, John. 'We're the Planners Now', *Guardian* (5 July 1971)

17 Hillman, Judy. 'A Plan Blessed and Scuppered', *Guardian* (16 Jan 1973)

18 Roberts, Nesta. 'Beaujolais and Bawdry', *Guardian* (1971)

19 *Liverpool Prospects*, the 1970 Report on City Objectives and Policies, 52–3

20 See, for instance, Prest, A. R. and Turvey, R. 'Cost Benefit Analysis, A Survey', *Economic Journal*, No 300 (1965), 683–731; and Lichfield, Nathanial. 'Evaluation Techniques, A Review Article', *Regional Studies*, 4 (1970), 140–65, which contains a very full bibliography of the subject.

21 I am throughout using the word 'value' in its philosophical sense of 'a state or condition that a person desires to attain' and not in its sociological one of 'social norms', which may reflect rather what people are *allowed* or have been *conditioned* to want. My definition links 'values' strongly to 'wants'. The sociological one is more concerned with observed behaviour.

22 Foley, Donald. 'An Approach to Metropolitan Spatial Structure' in Webber, M. (ed). *Explorations into Urban Structure* (New York 1964)

23 McLoughlin, J. B. *Urban and Regional Planning, A Systems Approach* (1969), particularly Chapter 9 'System Simulation, Forecasting and Modelling'

24 Charmayeff, S. and Alexander, C. *Community and Privacy* (1966)

5   HOW NOT TO DO IT (pp 72–95)

1   *Housing Return for England and Wales,* Cmnd 3068 (30 June 1966), 4, Table 4

2   Le Corbusier, *City of Tomorrow* (Paris 1924, translated and reprinted London, 1947) particularly Chapter 11, 'A Contemporary City for Three Million Inhabitants'. See also ref 1, Chapter 4. For an eloquent critique see Jane Jacobs. *Death and Life of Great American Cities* (New York 1961, reprinted London 1964)

3   Stone, P. A. *Urban Development in Britain: Costs, Standards, and Resources, 1964–2004,* Vol I (1970), 121. Table 7.11 'Price levels of flatted blocks by number of storeys, 31 March, 1964'

4   Stewart, W. F. R. *Children in Flats, A Family Study,* National Society for the Prevention of Cruelty to Children (1970), 22

5   Stewart, 26

6   Jephcott, Pearl. *Homes in High Flats* (Edinburgh, 1971), 59–79

7   Jephcott, 81

8   Jephcott, 131

9   Best, R. H. 'The Future of Urban Acreage', *Town and Country Planning,* Vol 32, Nos 8 & 9 (1964)

10   Stone. P. A. *Housing, Town Development, Land and Costs* (1963)

11   Best, 'The Future of Urban Acreage'

12   Midland Bank. *Britain's Agriculture To-day* (1968), 7 and 8, Tables 2 & 3

13   Before a change in government policy in 1968 the extra subsidy could amount to as much as £30 a year for 60 years, or a total of £1,800 a dwelling (Jephcott, 17)

14   The Local Government Boundary Commission in England will undertake 'a periodic general review of areas, and boundary adjustments will be made from time to time . . . for instance, bringing suburbs into a city district'. Ardill, John. 'Fresh strengths for 278 districts', *Guardian,* 27 April 1972

15   Stone. *Urban Development in Britain,* 214–15

16   *Town and Country Planning Act* (1968), Section 8 (1)

17   In Leeds shops in the precinct have increased their trade by an average of 24 per cent, compared with 4 per cent for those outside (Michael Parkin. 'Stroller Streets One Snag', *Guardian,* 19 April 1972). Stockholm is planning to build more precincts that will be crossed only by buses, following the success of those already operating in Vallingby suburb (Judy Hillman. 'Fare Games', *Guardian,* 10 October 1971)

18   Supported by sample surveys, 1970 and 1971 in Merseyside and Caernarvonshire taken by students in Liverpool Polytechnic's Department of Town and Country Planning

19   Liverpool, which has spent several millions of pounds on acquisition of the site for its New St John's Shopping Precinct, has recently imposed a 5 per cent cut back on its educational and social services programmes

20   Bob Dumbleton. 'Hook Road Cardiff', *Community Action,* 1 (Feb 1972), 19

21   Hall, Peter. *The World Cities* (1966), 37, 205

22   Webber, Melvin. 'Planning in An Environment of Change', Part 11,

'Permissive Planning', *Town Planning Review*, 39, No 4 (Jan 1969), 293

23 Councillor E. Roderick, quoted in 'Now for the "leave your car at home" drive', *Liverpool Weekly News* (10 August 1972)
24 Willmott, Peter, and Young, Michael, 'How Urgent are London's Motorways', *New Society*, 428 (Dec 1970), 1036
25 Holmes, E. H. (Director of Planning, US Bureau of Public Roads, Washington). 'Looking 25 years ahead in Highway Development in the United States', the Sixth Rees Jeffries Triennial Lecture to the Town Planning Institute (London 1965), 20
26 Willmott, and Young. 'How Urgent are London's Motorways?', 1037
27 Lindsay, John. *The City*
28 Hansen, N. 'French National Planning Experience', *Journal of the Institute of American Planners* (Nov 1969)
29 I am indebted for this information to my former colleague David Leyland, who worked on the Chelmsley Wood development as an architect planner for a number of years
30 This process of continually regrouping the members of organisations into teams appropriate for the changing tasks in hand is recommended by Donald Schon, *Beyond the Stable State* (1971). The alternative, and currently very fashionable, approach is the Programme Planning and Budgeting System, which creates a formal cycle of information circulation between departments. Each department defines objectives and analyses alternative programmes, which are then circulated and amended to coordinate with others, before each is allocated funds. The cycle is repeated each year, in theory ensuring coordination. In practice, each department protects its own cherished projects, and insists that *others* adapt to meet *its* priorities

6 HOMES (pp 96–120)

1 Abrams, Charles. *Man's Struggle for Shelter in an Urbanizing World* (Boston, 1964, reprinted London 1966 as *Housing in the Modern World*)
2 *Handbook of Statistics* (Local Government, Housing and Planning) (1970)
3 For USA, see, for example, Judy Hillman. 'Crack-up cities', *Guardian* (1971) and Glazer, Nathan.'The Renewal of Cities', *Cities*, a *Scientific American* Book (New York, 1965, reprinted London 1967)
4 Morris, A. E. J. 'Industrialized Building, The Soviet Union', *Official Architecture and Planning*, 29, No 5 (1966). See also Abrams. *Housing in the Modern World*, Chapter 17, Section 2. 'The Position of the USSR Compared', 276–85
5 For Paris, see Hall, Peter. *The World Cities* (1966), 63 and 76
6 For the developing nations see Abrams, Charles. 'The Uses of Land in Cities', *Cities*, a *Scientific American* book, 136
7 Ministry of Housing and Local Government. *Old Houses into New Homes* (1968), 16, Table 1, and Table 6
8 See 'Poverty and the Labour Government', *Poverty*, No 3 (1970), 7

9   Stone, P. A. *Urban Development in Britain: Standards, Costs and Resources 1964–2004* (1970), 149–50, and 227

10 Abrams, 63–5 and 165–9, relates unsuccessful experiments in pre-fabrication to attempts to emulate the technological advance of the West

11 Stone, 227

12 Comment made by Miss M. L. Collins, Social Development Officer of Runcorn New Town Development Corporation (8 December 1971)

13 'Collapse of Newsham Tower Flats', *New Society* 295 (1968), 758. In March 1972 a similar occurrence resulted in the deaths of twelve people in Barcelona (*Guardian* captioned photograph, 7 March 1972)

14 These have mostly been connected with conversion of appliances to natural gas.

15 Stone, 149

16 Land prices still constitute in most parts of Britain a quarter or less of the final selling price of a house, and only in the south-east, where the housing shortage is most acute, do they reach a third. See 'Housing', *New Society*, No 511 (1972) 79–80

17 Davidoff, Paul and Linda, and Gold, Niel. 'Suburban Action: Advocate Planning for an Open Society', *Journal of the American Institute of Planners* (Jan 1970), 12–18

18 Hillman, Judy, 'Crack-up Cities', *Guardian* (1971)

19 Central Statistical Office. *Social Trends*, No 2 (1971), 131, Table 105

20 The new rents will be fixed on the basis of market values minus scarcity effects by unelected Scrutiny Committees, consisting mainly of lawyers, valuers and surveyors.

21 *Social Trends*, 131

22 Ministry of Housing and Local Government. *Old Houses into New Homes* (1967), 28, Table 13

23 *Handbook of Statistics* (1970), Table 18

24 'Grants soar to cover ¼M homes', *Guardian* (3 Oct 1972)

25 For rate of house building see *Handbook of Statistics*, 8, Table 11

26 Young, M. and Willmot, P. *Family and Kinship in East London* (1957, reprinted 1969), and Mays, J. and Vereker. *Urban Redevelopment and Planning*

27 Needleman, L. 'The Comparative Economics of Improvement and New Building', *Urban Studies*, Vol 6, No 2 (1969), 199

28 Raphael, Adam. 'Housing scandals embarrass Nixon', *Guardian* (26 April 1972)

29 *Social Trends*, Table 98

30 Jacobs, Jane. *Death and Life of Great American Cities* (1961, reprinted 1965)

31 Office of Population and Census Surveys. *Census, 1971, England and Wales: Preliminary Report*

32 Stone, 211

33 *Handbook of Statistics* (1970), 9, Table 12

34 *Social Trends* (1971), 124, Table 89

35 Young and Willmott. *Family and Kinship in East London*, 128

36 In the New Town of Dronten in the Netherlands national government funds were used to construct and subsidise up to a level of £30,000 a year a multi-purpose recreational and cultural centre

named the 'Agora' after the focal point of ancient Greek cities. (Information from Drs Venstra, Director of the Rijksdienst voor de Ijsselmeerpolders. and from personal research)

37 Moser, Claus. 'Measuring the Quality of Life', *New Society*, No 428 (1970) 1042–5

38 Dr W. V. Hole and J. J. Attenburrow of the Building Research Station. *Houses and People, A Review of User Studies* (1966), deals systematically with people's uses and needs in the home, and summarises a decade of similar published work done at the BRS. Their work has been largely ignored so far in the design of new public housing.

39 Morris, Rosalind. *Guardian* (29 July 1971)

40 Hillman, Judy. 'New Town's Bright Future', *Guardian* (28 April 1972)

41 *Housing Statistics*, 23 (1971), 64, Table 57

42 Crosland, Anthony. *Towards a Labour Housing Policy* (1971), 3–4. Stone, 177, also points to the growing demand for second homes.

43 Lindsay, John. *The City*, 125

44 Lambeth Public Relations Officer. *Lambeth Housing: A New Concept* (1971)

45 *Lambeth Housing: A New Concept*, 2

7 PHYSICAL COMMUNICATIONS (pp 121–37)

1 See John Ardill. 'Census shows nearly one million people have left conurbations', *Guardian* (19 August 1971). In New York alone the Regional Plan Association's Harvard Study estimates that in the period 1960–85 the city itself and other inner areas will lose 446,000 residents, while the new exurbanite zone will gain more than 4 million people. See Hall, Peter. *The World Cities* (1966), 213–16

2 The GLC estimates that the 30 miles of Ringway 1 (60 per cent of which would be elevated) would involve the destruction of about 8,000 dwellings. (Thompson, J. Michael. *Motorways in London*, 1969, 130).

3 Webber, Melvin. 'The Urban Place and the Non Place Urban Realm' in Webber (ed). *Explorations into Urban Structure* (New York 1964)

4 British Railways Board. *Reshaping British Railways* (The Beeching Report, 1963)

5 Hall, P. 'What is a motorway?', *New Society*, 479 (1971), 1094

6 For world vehicle production statistics, see *Oxford Economic Atlas of the World*, 4th ed (1972), 55

7 For examples of pressure applied by the motor lobby, see British Road Federation. *Highway Needs* (1971), *Road User Taxation and Road Investment: A Pre-Budget Memorandum* (1967), *Where Are the Motorways?* (1967) *and Finance and Roads* (1972)

8 Thompson, J. Michael. *Motorways in London* (1969), 141

9 Thompson, 109, 118–20

10 Walters, A. A. 'Road Pricing' in Munby, E. (ed). *Transport (Penguin Modern Economics)* 184–211. See also Ministry of Transport. *Road*

Pricing: Economic and Technical Possibilities (The Smeed Report, 1964)

11 Holmgren, Per. 'Integration of Public Transport with Urban Development', *Report of Proceedings of Town and Country Planning Summer School* (1965)

12 Homan, Richard. 'Traffic free stroll enchants the city of Strauss', *Guardian* (19 Jan 1972)

13 *Social Trends* (1971), 137, Table 113

14 *Social Trends* (1971), 137

15 Thompson. *Motorways in London*, 11

16 Carson-Parker. 'U.S. taxpayers get railroaded', *Observer* (7 May 1972). Following the collapse of the Penn Central Railway the US government established 'Amtrak', a national rail corporation, with an initial annual subsidy of $250 million. A similar sum has been wiped by government off British Rail's debt burden. See Keegan, V. *Guardian* (28 July 1972)

17 Dykman. J. W. 'Transportation in Cities', *Cities*, a *Scientific American* Book (New York 1965, reprinted London 1967), 156–66. See also Raphael, Adam. 'Take a train into the 21st century', *Guardian* (26 March 1970)

18 Raphael, Adam. 'Highways alone will not solve U.S. traffic jams', *Guardian* (25 March 1971)

19 Fairhall. John. 'The happy band of travellers', *Guardian* (23 July 1971)

20 Holmgren

21 Picquard, Michel. 'Regional Planning in France', *Proceedings of the Town and Country Planning Summer School* (1967), 36. A 156 miles long regional express railroad network is at present nearing completion

22 In Rotterdam the new rail links new southern residential estates to the city centre with a rapid and frequent service.

23 Thompson, 16

24 Jenkins, R. C. *Transport and Traffic Management in Reading*, cyclostyled report produced by Reading's Transport Manager (1972)

25 Bendixson, Terence. 'Fare Games', *Guardian* (5 Oct 1971)

26 Reuter. 'Omnibus gratis (pro tem)', *Guardian* (31 Dec 1971)

27 Jacobs, Jane. *Death and Life of Great American Cities* (New York 1961, reprinted London 1965)

28 See, for instance, Brzezinski, Z. 'America in the Technetronic Age'. *Encounter*, 30, No 1 (1968), and Webber, M. 'The Urban Place and the Non Place Urban Realm' in *Explorations into Urban Structure*

29 Dunning, J. H. 'The City of London, A Case Study in Urban Economics', *Town Planning Review*, 40, No 3 (1969). 230

30 Alexander, Christopher.' The City is not a Tree', *Design*, 206 (1967), 46–55

31 Allison. J. R. 'A Method of Analysis of the Pedestrian System of a Town Centre,' *Journal of the Town Planning Institute*, 56, No 8, 352–6

32 Allison, 352

8 *CITIES AND TOWNS* (pp 138–52)

1 The Inland Town was founded by settlers who crossed the Niger from the west 150–200 years ago. As one of the many tragic results of the recent Nigerian Civil War much of the Inland Town, as described in this chapter, no longer exists.

2 Industry has instead developed in the nearby towns of Padua, Treviso and Vicenza, for which Venice is the port. Petroleum storage and refining takes place at Mestre 3 miles away on the mainland. The fact that the whole superb city is now threatened with rapid subsidence into the surrounding sea has been traced to the scouring effect of the backwash of the huge oiltankers on their way through the lagoon to Mestre.

3 Mumford, Lewis. *The City in History* (New York 1961, reprinted London 1968), Section 9 of Chapter 14, 'Amsterdam's Exemplary Contrast'

4 Richards, J. M. *Modern Architecture* (1940, revised and reprinted 1962), 87, 109–10. Richards speaks of his 'precise, logical studies in pure geometry' (87), and describes them as 'masterpieces of precise engineering' (110).

5 Morris, A. E. J. 'Habitat 67', *Official Architecture and Planning*, 30, No 6 (1967). The Israeli architect Moshe Safdie's design to accommodate workers at the 1967 Montreal World Expo achieved both high densities and provision of private open space by arranging dwellings so that the roof of one provided the 'garden' of another.

6 See Cohen, Gerda. 'In sickness and in hope', *Guardian* (20 June 1972). She refers to 'Gale swept concrete cuboids . . . rheumatic sludge . . . grey plateau suspended over the car park, lugubrious with wind and sodden litter . . . murky channels which appear part of the nearby sewage treatment works . . . chill gangways between densely curtained kitchen windows'.

7 Martienssen, Rex. *The Idea of Space in Greek Architecture* (1947)

8 Mumford, Lewis. *The City in History*, particularly Chapter 10, 'Medieval Urban Housekeeping'

9 For a particularly good discussion see Mumford

10 Such a viewpoint is well satirised by Charles Dickens in *Hard Times* (1854, reprinted regularly) and Upton Sinclair's *The Jungle* (1906, reprinted 1965). The former is set in Manchester, and the latter in Chicago.

11 Sitte, Camillo. *City Planning According to Artistic Principles* (1899, translated and reprinted 1965)

12 Lynch, Kevin. *The Image of the City* (Cambridge, Mass, 1960, reprinted 1971)

13 Lynch, 32

14 Lynch, 155

15 Predictably hailed by Richards, *Modern Architecture*, as carrying 'yet another stage further, the combination of imaginative form and technical sophistication for which Brazil was already noted'. (108) A shanty town has grown up to house the many thousands of workers who cannot afford to live in the new show buildings.

9   QUANTITY AND QUALITY (pp 153–75)

1   This problem was given its classic formulation by C. P. Snow, the scientist and novelist, in the Rede Lecture entitled 'The Two Cultures' in 1953.

2   Skinner, B. F. *Beyond Freedom and Dignity* (New York 1972)

3   Eliot, T. S. *Notes Towards a Definition of Culture* (1948, reprinted 1962)

4   Williams, Raymond. *Culture and Society* (1960) contains a devastating critique of Eliot's elitist position.

5   Pemberton, W. B. *William Cobbett* (1949), 106–7. Wilberforce's hypocrisy led Cobbett to refer to him as 'that great canter and noise-maker about humanity'.

6   *Oxford Economic Atlas* (1972), 118, and *Social Trends* (1972), 159

7   One example was *Containerization and the future of British Ports*, commissioned from McKinsey Incorporated, the Management Consultants (1968). The report suggested that only Tilbury as a port had a long term future, and was based on deep ignorance of the reasons for the growth and success of the ports of Liverpool, Hull and Southampton. Port planners ignored the report, and Liverpool is now rightly being developed as the country's major container port.

8   Both the South-east Lancashire and North-east Cheshire and the Merseyside Area Land Use Transportation Studies cost more than £300,000 (or nearly a million dollars) each. In the former case the consultants, W. S. Atkins, Ltd, felt unable to finish the work without further funds.

9   Henri, A., McGough, R., Patten, B. *The Mersey Sound* (1967), 85

10   Fuller. R. B. *Utopia or Oblivion* (1971), quoted in Comfort, Alex. 'Nasty, technological and long', *Guardian* (1971)

11   Sharp, Dennis. 'The stage beyond the city', *Guardian* (29 August 1970)

12   Doxiadis, C. *Ekistics, An Introduction to the Science of Human Settlements* (1968). A monthly magazine called *Ekistics* is also published

13   Veblen, Thorstein. *The Theory of the Leisure Class* (1899). See also Packard, Vance. *The Waste Makers* (1965)

14   Wilsher, Peter. 'Hell on earth for the sons of heaven', *Observer* (19 Dec 1971)

15   Social priorities for Japan', *Guardian* (18 Jan 1972)

16   Arnstein, Sherry. 'A Ladder of Citizen Participation in the U.S.A.', *Journal of the Royal Town Planning Institute*, 57, No 4 (1971), 176–82

17   Arnstein, 177

18   Roberts, Nesta. 'Beaujolais and Bawdry', *Guardian* (1971)

19   See, for instance, Anderson, Martin. *The Federal Bulldozer* (Cambridge, Mass, 1964), particularly Chapter Ten

20   See, for instance, Howard. 'Garden Cities of Tomorrow (1902, reprinted 1946); Geddes, Patrick. *Cities in Evolution* (1915, reprinted 1949); and Mairet, Philip. *Pioneer of Sociology, the life and Letters of Patrick Geddes* (1957)

21   During the late 1960s planning powers, designed to improve social welfare, were misused to make financial profits for city corporations

and developers. One signal of the retreat from this form of legalised exploitation was F. J. C. Amos's Presidential Address in October 1971 to the Royal Town Planning Institute, *Journal of the Royal Town Planning Institute*, 57, No 9 (1971) 398, in which he pleaded for 'planners who are sufficiently free from economic pressures and loyalty to clients or employers to plead the cause of the deprived and the disadvantaged . . . .'

22 Carmichael, Stokely, and Hamilton, Charles V. *Black Power, The Politics of Liberation in America* (New York 1967), 156
23 Glazer, Nathan. 'The Renewal of Cities', *Cities*, a *Scientific American* Book (New York 1965, reprinted London 1967), 193–202
24 I am indebted for use of this vivid phrase to Dr Andreas Faludi, who coined it in his article 'The Planning Environment and the Meaning of Planning', *Regional Studies* (May 1970).
25 Young, Michael, and Willmott, Peter. 'How Urgent are London's Motorways?', *New Society*, No 428 (1970), 1036–8
26 Amos, F. J. C. 'Presidential Address', *Journal of the Royal Town Planning Institute*, 57, No 9, 399
27 In the Netherlands, for instance, any group able to muster 50,000 supporting signatories has some time each month to present its own programmes on the national television network. In the USA the Office of Economic Opportunity programmes are all based on citizen participation. In Britain the Skeffington Report, *People and Planning* (1969), and Sections 3 and 7 of the 1968 *Town and Country Planning Act* deal with the rights of local people to have their say at the formative planning stages.
28 Hill, Dilys. *Participating in Local Affairs* (1970), 38–40
29 Henderson, A. 'Airport Planning and Transport Systems', and Newson, G. E. 'The Sheppey Study, The Original Concept', *Official Architecture and Planning*, 30 No 2, 208–9 and 219–21
30 Hall, Peter. 'Roskill's Felicific Calculus', *New Society*, 386 (1970), 306–8
31 Jacobs. *Death and Life of Great American Cities*, 311, and Alinsky, Saul D. *Reveille for Radicals*
32 Beard, Andy. 'Cardiff Residents Beat Town and Gown', *Community Action*, 2 (1972)
33 Information from John Taylor, first secretary of West End Tenants' Association
34 Hillmore, Peter. 'The gamble in the empty spaces', *Guardian* (5 May 1972). See also Hillman, Judy. '£100M scheme to change the face of Piccadilly Circus', *Guardian* (3 May 1972)
35 Richards, J. M. 'How to kill Piccadilly Circus', and Silver, Nathan. 'Coventry Street, WI', *The Listener*, 87 No 2255 (1972), 777–80
36 Hillman, Judy. 'Growth in the Jungle', *Guardian* (1 August 1972)
37 Hillman, Judy. 'Down to size', *Guardian* (1971)
38 Wilsher, Peter. 'Hell on earth for sons of heaven', *Sunday Times* (19 Dec 1971)
39 Wilson, Des. 'The facts Heath won't reveal', *Observer* (27 Feb 1972)
40 'Tunnel troubles at Bath', *Guardian* (22 Jan 1972)
41 Lindsay, John. *The City* (New York 1969, reprinted London 1971)
42 Trimborn, Harry. 'Solzhenitsyn accuses KGB', *Guardian* (16 August 1971)

Index

190